LOST IN FLORENCE

An insider's guide to the best places to eat, drink and explore

NARDIA PLUMRIDGE

TRAVEL

LOST IN FLORENCE

*An insider's guide to the best places
to eat, drink and explore*

NARDIA PLUMRIDGE

CONTENTS

NINE

171

DAYTRIP ITINERARIES

WELCOME TO
LOST IN FLORENCE

Benvenuto!

My love affair with Florence is long, and Lost in Florence *came to life
with a desire to showcase the 'chic, boutique, and unique' venues in the
Renaissance capital. Incredible places run by passionate artisans of style
or food, spaces tucked away from the crowds, found by turning down an
innocuous cobbled street to discover a hole-in-the-wall eatery or boutique
store run by friendly locals. Often the best Florence experiences are when
we take that unexpected turn and get lost ... in the most adventurous sense.*

*I first visited Tuscany at age 15 and was immediately mesmerised by
Florence's beauty, its graceful buildings and open piazze which are
museum-like, filled with elegant statues and bordered by cafes with locals
lounging al fresco sipping cappuccini well into the late morning sunshine.
That trip I vowed to return when I was older, to live for a summer, which
I did, finally, in 2010. I packed up my London flat, bought a one-way
ticket and spent year-end immersed in the city. I took art classes, drank
cappuccini well into the late morning sunshine and soaked in the unique
spirit this city holds – a certain 'dolce vita' that washes over you and there,
just like that, you're hooked. Years on, my passion for the city remains
ignited.*

*I have discovered most people are searching for Italy's famous 'sweet
life', craving more than just gelato or Michelangelo's David (although he
is rather handsome and worth seeing). This book combines my passion
for Florence with its people and places to take you on a journey through
its ancient streets. I share hidden venues and guide you on itineraries to
discover your own unforgettable adventure.*

Are you ready to be Lost in Florence *too?*

Buon viaggio!
Nardia

ABOUT FLORENCE

Florence today is a magnificent example of Renaissance architecture built on the wealth of the city's 15th- and 16th-century burgeoning new banking scene, as the newly rich built grand palazzi (palaces) to out-do their neighbours and commissioned fine artworks by the city's most talented creatives to adorn their palace walls.

Florence's history dates back to Roman times with an early settlement 'Florentia' by the river Arno during the reign of Julius Caesar. The Roman town was laid out in typical grid-like Roman fashion, its main crossroad is today marked by a pillar with a grey sandstone statue of Dovizia atop Colonna dell'Abbondanza, in Piazza della Repubblica, and noted by street names like Via Roma (the road leading south towards Rome). During the Middle Ages, Florence became a hub for the textile industry making many citizens wealthy and the city became a centre of European life. These riches enabled families to diversify into other businesses, namely banking, when the Renaissance period really took off.

The city's most famous family are the Medici, bankers, art patrons, private citizens and Grand Dukes who ruled the walled city, in politics and business, from Cosimo de'Medici's reign from 1434, through Lorenzo Il Magnifico, 'The Magnificent', until their eventual demise in 1737 (I recommend The Medici Dynasty Show, see p.157, to understand all this history in one short hour). During the end of the Medici reign, it was the lesser known Anna Maria Luisa who, with her brother, created the Family Pact instilling the condition in her will that all the art and collections of the Medici dynasty remain in her beloved Florence, which it still does today; it's what makes the city the best preserved Renaissance capital in the world.

During the city's Renaissance heyday, Florence was divided into four different quartiere – Santa Croce, Santo Spirito, Santa Maria Novella and San Giovanni – which still make up the four teams for the annual calico storico (historic soccer) matches played in Piazza Santa Croce each June. Yet the city has more than four central neighbourhoods, many still retaining a village-like charm, all of which are worth exploring.

About

ABOUT FLORENCE

Up until 1865, Florence was a walled city surrounded by ten-metre-tall stone mure (walls) and entered into via sixteen porte (gates). When the city was gentrified after Italy's unification in 1860, the council wished to modernise the city and feeling that old medieval walls were, well, old, they knocked them down on the north side of Florence to make way for sweeping boulevards – tree-lined streets, known as Viale, fashioned on the streets of Paris, the city du jour of the time.

The city's heart lies within the old Renaissance parameters, intersected by the river Arno, crossed by the famed Ponte Vecchio bridge, and containing the major landmarks: the Uffizi Gallery, Palazzo Pitti, Boboli Gardens, Galleria dell'Accademia, Palazzo Vecchio and the Duomo. And not to forget the vista from Piazzale Michelangelo to watch the sun set over the city's famed terracotta rooftops. Florence has so much to discover, from classic art to contemporary exhibitions, plus an illustrious heritage for fashion and food. It's a city to ignite your passions on every level.

For a small city of just over 300,000 residents, Florence is a vibrant capital that today retains much of its traditions especially with its artisan heritage. Equally, there is a burgeoning array of contemporary spaces and places to enjoy a happy balance of traditionally made creative crafts with a modern design twist, whether it's leather-made goods or jewellery in artisan studios, or restaurants using locally sourced produce of the finest quality. And lest we forget we are in wine country – Florence is surrounded by some of the finest vineyards in Italy and is just a skip from the famed Chianti region, with the city boasting a number of beautiful boutique wine bars.

FLORENCE

Key

1. *David* and the
   Galleria dell'Accademia
2. Duomo
3. Palazzo Vecchio
4. Basilica di Santa Croce
5. Uffizi Gallery
6. Ponte Vecchio
7. Palazzo Pitti
8. Forte di Belvedere

SANTA MARIA NOVELLA

ARNO

SAN FREDIANO

SANTO SPIRITO

SAN LORENZO

0   200M

SANT'AMBROGIO

SAN GIOVANNI

SANTA CROCE

ARNO

SAN NICCOLÒ

NEIGHBOURHOOD INDEX

NEIGHBOURHOOD INDEX

NOTABLE
NEIGHBOURHOODS

All of the key landmarks and places to visit in Florence are perfectly positioned within the parameters of the old city walls, even if most of the old stone doesn't exist today, with the city cut into two (north and south) by the river Arno. Throughout this book, I've divided Florence's historic centre into eight key neighbourhoods, highlighting the best places to eat, drink, and shop. Here's a short summary of each.

NORTH OF THE ARNO

SAN GIOVANNI
—

At the centre of Florence, San Giovanni's most famous landmark is the must-see cathedral, the Duomo (see p.145), or by official title, Cathedral di Santa Maria del Fiore. Its impressive dome, lined with terracotta tiles, designed by Filippo Brunelleschi in the 15th century, is a beacon for the city. This neighbourhood is the centre of Florence with many shopping, dining and wine spots within the city's three main squares: Piazza della Signoria, Piazza della Repubblica, and Piazza del Duomo. From here the other central neighbourhoods north of the Arno radiate outwards and you will find a bustling energy from both locals and tour groups alike. Climbing to the top of the dome is a popular exercise (quite literally), though book online for your time slot to guarantee entry.

SANTA MARIA NOVELLA
—

To the Duomo's west, the Piazza of Santa Maria Novella is lined with elegant hotels and eateries offering al fresco dining, their seats looking towards the marble facade of the church. Streets like Via del Moro and Via dei Fossi shine and are ideal for window-shopping antiques and fashion or finding a Tuscan trattoria like Trattoria Sostanza (see p.199) to indulge in local fare. Florence's famous perfume house, Officina Profumo-Farmaceutica di Santa Maria Novella (see p.179), is close by, as is the city's main train station Stazione di Santa Maria Novella.

SAN LORENZO

–

To the north, San Lorenzo languished for years as the poor cousin to more elegant Santa Croce, yet in recent times an explosion of new bars, concept stores and dining options have made it a worthy go-to, especially come nightfall. The renovation of 19th-century food emporium, Il Mercato Centrale (see p.67), started this gentrification. By day, the mercato's surrounding streets off Via dell'Ariento host the San Lorenzo street-markets (see p.172), with stalls selling tourist trinkets and Florence's famed leather goods en masse. Come night, bars like Sabor Cubano (see p.190) or La Ménagère (see p.37) make it a neighbourhood worth lingering in.

SANTA CROCE

–

Its streets are crowded with leather stores, a hark back to the neighbourhood's original guise, and today Santa Croce remains popular with travellers who venture to its crown jewel, the 13th-century Basilica di Santa Croce in its main piazza housing the tombs of Florence glitterarti, including Michelangelo, Galileo and Machiavelli. Tucked within the church cloisters is Scuola del Cuoio (see p.109), known as the Leather School of Florence with a shop selling leather bookmarks through to handcrafted handbags. Via dei Benci by day is a pleasant mix of fashion and food outlets, and come night this street is awash with students, both local and foreign, eager for a night out on the city's cobbled tiles.

SANT'AMBROGIO

–

Further east the tempo becomes more local with Sant'Ambrogio a lesser travelled area of Florence and one that retains a village-like charm. Its market (see p.172) is a bustling morning affair with fruit and vegetable vendors, cheese mongers and butchers, while the piazza is lined with cafes and eateries whose chefs grab their daily produce at the market early before rustling up traditional Tuscan dishes for lunch. Cibréo Caffé (see p.43) brims with locals sipping a morning coffee between errands, its terrace a sun-blessed feature in the summer months.

SOUTH OF THE ARNO - OLTRARNO

SANTO SPIRITO
–

With its bohemian feel, Santo Spirito is a lively neighbourhood popular with students and locals alike who congregate on the church steps and in the piazza, drinking wine and eating pizza as the sun sets on another glorious Florence day. It also has a heady nightlife that has grown in recent years to include some fine cocktail bars. Its cultural stops are Palazzo Pitti (see p.163), where a day can easily be lost within its many ornate rooms, and its luscious greenery, Boboli Gardens (see p.184). Santo Spirito church is a simpler affair – its exterior is a clean, white-washed facade, however within you'll find an ornate baroque interior with a side room housing a 'secret' Michelangelo sculpture. The streets of this neighbourhood are filled with fine artisan botteghe (workshops) and Via di Santo Spirito is a must-do wander for window-shopping with wine stops along the way. Via Maggio has become an eclectic mix of old antiques and contemporary fashion.

SAN FREDIANO
–

In Oltrarno's west, San Frediano is the lesser visited sister to Santo Spirito but worth venturing into as the crowds from Ponte Vecchio start to dissipate and you'll find a heady mix of new openings that have infiltrated its little laneways. Discover the magnificent gallery/studio of Galleria Romanelli (see p.166) and the frescoes within Santa Maria church in Piazza del Carmine. Eating options are around Piazza Tasso, or try the €10 lunch menu at nearby L'Brindellone (see p.199) for a truly Tuscan food experience.

SAN NICCOLÒ
–

With just a few streets making up this neighbourhood, backing onto the medieval walls of Florence, San Niccolò is a quiet and quaint respite to the frenetic action across the river. At the crossroads of Via di San Niccolò and Via San Miniato you'll find little clusters of chairs and tables on the street are the ideal spot come aperitivo hour. Make time to pop into the gallery/studio of Alessandro Dari (see p.137) and Clet Abraham (see p.167) for a respectively old and new artisan experience, as each studio is, creatively, centuries apart. For the strong willed, walk the steep olive tree-lined street of Via di Belvedere by the old walls towards Forte di Belvedere (see p.169), open in the summer with contemporary sculpture on show and offering some of the city's most stunning views.

ON A SUNNY DAY

FULL DAY ITINERARY

Florence is an open-air museum, and this itinerary takes you from breakfast in Sant' Ambrogio, through culturual landmarks in the historic centre, to discover the other side of the river Arno. Visit palazzo, ponte and forte, fitting in delicious food stops and boutique shops along the way.

8.30AM Breakfast like a local at ① **Cibréo Caffé** (see p.43) in the residential neighbourhood of Sant'Ambrogio. Its outside terrace is ideal to sip a cappuccino and watch the locals going about their morning routine. For early risers, peruse the food, flowers and homewares in the neighbouring market of the same name.

10AM Allow yourself time to stroll through the streets of Santa Croce and admire its leather stores and 700 year-old church. Take Via dei Macci then turn right on Via San Giuseppe. Pop into ② **Scuola Del Cuoio** (see p.109) at number 5r. Through a discreet arch, follow the signs around the Santa Croce church apse to a quiet courtyard where artisans work under exposed brick arches. While inside the main building, go in search of leather trinkets. Next, head south with the piazza on your right, then turn on to Borgo Santa Croce to explore the rooms at perfume house ③ **Aqua Flor** (see p.111).

10.30AM Meander the laneways between Via dei Neri and Borgo dei Greci until you reach Piazza della Signoria. Admire the *David* statue, a copy dating from 1910 that overlooks the piazza then go in search of ④ **Palazzo Vecchio's** Lion House where Cosimo Medici the Elder kept his private collection of feline friends as attractions at festivities for visiting dignitaries. Begun in 1299, this medieval palace with its 94-meter high tower remains the political seat of Florence today (the mayor has his office here). Explore the stately room, Salone dei Cinquecento, created for the grand council of 500 members, and the old Medici apartments where the family lived until the mid-1500s. Don't forget to climb Arnolfo Tower for stunning views over Florence.

12PM Along Via Vaccereccia and onto Via Por Santa Maria, head south and cross the Arno over the famed ⑤ **Ponte Vecchio** with its glittering jewellery stores. Dating back to the 14th century, it's the oldest existing bridge in the city. Snap a quick picture by the bust of Cellini looking west towards Ponte Santa Trinita, then take a left turn up medieval Via de' Bardi. Pop into ⑥ **Il Torchio** at number 17 (see p.139), a heavenly paper shop run by artisan Erin Ciulla who handmakes the leather-bound books and marble effect paper. Further along on Via di San Niccolò visit ⑦ **Alessandro Dari's** bottega (at 115r; see p.137), a magical museum dedicated to his jewellery creations. For the street-art enthusiast, swing by ⑧ **Clet Abraham's** (see p.167) studio on the corner of Via dell'Olmo before heading into the heart of San Niccolò.

12.30PM Follow your nose on Via San Miniato which turns into Via del Monte alle Croci, you'll find a gate to enter and enjoy spectacular Florence views at ⑨ **Rose Garden** (see p.184), where entry is free. Tucked into the city's southern hills, this heavenly park has 400 varieties of roses and 12 modern sculptures by Belgian Jean-Michel Folon. In April and May the blooms are best, while its Japanese garden is an oasis all year.

1PM Nestle in for lunch by the 14th-century medieval walls at trattoria ⑩ **La Beppa Fioraia** (see p.91), at the beginning of the green parkland on Via dell'Erta Canina, its greenhouse setting bursting with natural light and overlooking lush parkland. The antipasti board of meats, cheese, condiments and coccoli (fried dough balls) are a speciality, as are the many handmade pasta dishes. In summer, sit in the garden, where the best tables are tucked between olive trees.

3PM Walk off lunch with a visit to ⑪ **Forte di Belvedere** (see p.169). Backtrack briefly along Via del Monte alle Croce, then take the steep ascent up Via di Belvedere lined with olive trees beside the medieval walls then explore the Forte grounds. Built for the Medici in the 1590s, this former fortress is now a summer space offering iconic annual art exhibitions in its gardens. However, it's the views that are the main attraction. Open until 8pm in summer, its bar is an optimal spot for a pre-dinner cocktail.

6.30PM Stroll back towards town on Costa San Giorgio taking a left onto Via de' Guicciardini at Piazza Santa Felicita then a right on Via dello Sprone. Pop into ⑫ **Sara Amrhein's** (at 9r; see p.125) colourful studio to peruse her statement jewellery then browse the international magazine collection on sale at ⑬ **Bjørk** (at 25r; see p.119). At the end of Via dello Sprone, head south along Via Maggio, taking a right onto Via dei Michelozzi.

7.30PM Dine al fresco in Piazza Santo Spirito with a number of eateries spilling into the leafy square. ⑭ **Tamerò's** (see p.85) interior retains much of the gritty feel of its previous guise as a mechanic's workshop, however, its outside seats gracing the quaint piazza hold the most charm. An aperitivo buffet from 6.30pm means early dining birds can enjoy watching the sunset colours change on the facade of the square's 15th-century church in parts attributed to architect Filippo Brunelleschi.

Florence is a haven for indoor pursuits with an array of amazing art galleries and opulent interiors to explore, and seriously good food, so don't let the weather deter you. This itinerary will take you through historic San Giovanni to San Lorenzo, taking in iconic landmarks and sampling the best of classic Florentine food for lunch and dinner.

8AM Start your day with caffeine consumption on Via dei Neri at ① **Ditta Artigianale** (see p.39), choosing from simple espresso to three brewing methods. Or fill up on their pancakes, French toast, scrambled eggs or croque monsieur.

9AM Stroll up Via dei Neri past its array of panini joints and along Via dei Castellani towards the art museum of Florence, and the oldest public gallery in the world, ② **Uffizi Gallery** (see p.147), housing thousands of works by Michelangelo, Botticelli, Da Vinci, Raphael, Titian and Caravaggio, to name a few. It's one of the city's busiest spaces and a must-see for the first-time, or repeat traveller, however allow yourself ample time and choose which collections you wish to see. Tour groups flock to the Botticellis, however my recommendation is to seek the newly renovated red rooms in the east wing dedicated to Caravaggio and 17th-century painting. As the gallery is busy all year round, pre-booking your ticket is a must.

12.30PM Wander up Piazzale degli Uffizi and across Piazza della Signoria, past the statue of *Neptune* for lunch at hole-in-the-wall diner, ③ **Osteria Vini e Vecchi Sapori** (Via dei Magazzini 3r; see p.198). Choose from a list of traditional Tuscan dishes such as meaty ragu tossed with thick pappardelle, or try summer favourite bread soup, pappa al pomodoro. With just a handful of tables arrive before it fills with a hungry lunchtime crowd.

2.30PM Post lunch, stroll down Via della Condotta then take a left turn on Via del Proconsolo to explore the oldest public building in Florence. ④ **Bargello** (Via del Proconsolo 4) was home to the city council in the Middle Ages and later acted as a prison – up until 1786 executions still took place in the inner courtyard. Today it is a public gallery housing works by Michelangelo, Cellini and Donatello's *David*, a bronze cast commissioned by the Medici family. Beyond sculpture, seek out the armoury display plus discover a fine collection of ceramics, textiles, tapestries and antique coins.

4.30PM Head down Via del Proconsolo towards the city's imposing Duomo taking a left on Piazza del Duomo. Look out for the statue of architect Filippo Brunelleschi wistfully looking up towards his famous dome. Stroll across the street past the Duomo's imposing ⑤ **bell tower** designed by Giotto and completed in 1359. Use your €18 inclusive Il Grande Museo del Duomo ticket (see p.145) to climb the tower's 414 steps for panoramic city views 85 metres above the ground. Then head to ⑥ **Move On** (Via Piazza di San Giovanni 1r; see p.190), a record store and craft beer bar within a cosy wood-panelled room. Peruse vintage and new-release vinyl in their upstairs space, taking a peek from their windows which offer stunning views over the square towards the marble facade of the cathedral. Then descend the stairs to its ground floor bar to sample a selection of Italian beer on tap and order a plate of Tuscan cold cuts and local cheeses to match your drink.

6.30PM Head to the far side of Piazza di San Giovanni, then stroll down Borgo San Lorenzo past the bare brick neighbourhood church and take a left at Piazza San Lorenzo, continuing around the terracotta dome of the Medici Chapel before you arrive at Via Faenza. Head towards Il Fuligno to watch a pre-dinner performance of ⑦ **The Medici Dynasty Show** (see p.157) a riveting performance (and in English language) at 7pm. Performed in a deconsecrated baroque church and set in 1737, the play follows the last of the Medici family, siblings Gian Gastone and Anna Maria Luisa, who conceive a plan to save their family's legacy, plus precious works of art, from being sold off or leaving their beloved Florence. Detailing over 300 years of Florence's history in one action-packed hour.

8PM Post show delve into classic Tuscan cuisine on Via Nazionale at ⑧ **Braciere Malatesta** (see p.68), a family run trattoria using the same charcoal grill and wood-fire oven since the 1950s to turn out delicious plates of pasta or freshly baked pizza. A renovated vintage-style dining room is ideal for larger groups and with bistecca on the menu, it's a meat lovers' paradise.

10PM Enjoy a late night stroll down Via dell'Ariento, left onto Via Sant'Antonio to Via Taddea to ⑨ **La Ménagère** (see p.37), on Via de' Ginori, one of the hippest openings in recent years, it's a concept store personified: part cafe, restaurant, homewares shop and florist all under one roof. Order a cocktail off the creative drinks list then descend into the basement where jazz music is hosted for free four nights a week.

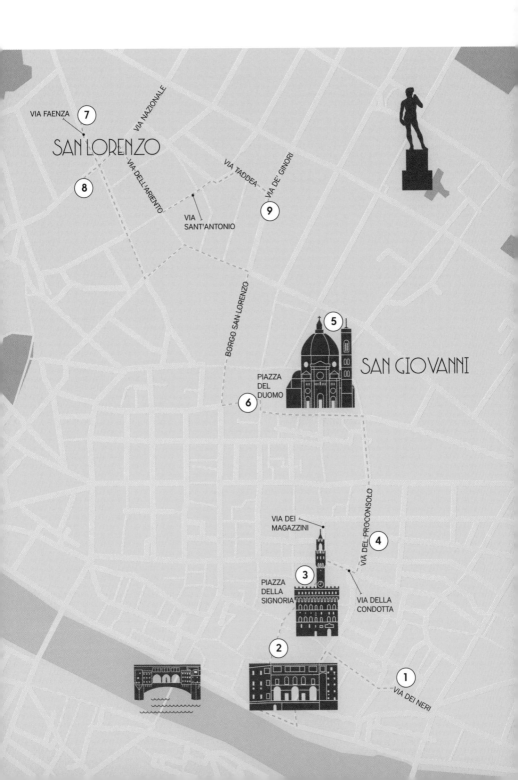

FLORENCE FOR FOODIES
FULL DAY ITINERARY

SAN LORENZO PIAZZA MERCATO
CENTRALE
①

SANTA MARIA
NOVELLA

③

②

VIA PELLICCERIA

VIA PORTA
ROSSA ④
⑤

SAN FREDIANO

⑥

VIA DI SANTO SPIRITO

SAN GIOVANNI

SANTO SPIRITO

VIA DEI
VELLUTI ⑩
⑧

⑨

VIA DEI SERRAGLI

VIA DELLE CALDAIE

VIA SANTA MARIA

⑦

Food and Florence go hand-in-hand and a trip to the Tuscan capital deserves savouring the local fare, celebrating the region's producers. Explore culinary delights from Il Mercato Centrale in San Lorenzo to a pasta masterclass and gelato to finish in Santo Spirito, with enough walking in between to keep your appetite going. Don't forget to pre-book your class at In Tavola.

8AM Start your morning in San Lorenzo at (1) **Il Mercato Centrale** (see p.67), the largest food market in Florence. Explore the stalls of vegetables, meats and cheese and sample balsamic vinegars and olive oils. For the strong-willed, join the locals ordering lamprodotto at Da Narbone, a tripe sandwich traditionally washed down with a glass of Chianti – even at 9am! Alternatively their boiled beef panini is succulent and delicious.

10AM Stroll the streets of San Lorenzo towards (2) **Piazza della Repubblica**, to the north-east of this pedestrian-only cobblestoned square for your cappuccino fix at (3) **Caffè Gilli** (see p.29). Indulge in frescoes and fluffy pastries at the marble bar, which is also the best spot to people watch.

11AM Head across the piazza, down Via Pellicceria, towards Via Porta Rossa and pop into (4) **Antonio Mattei Piccolo Museo Bottega** (at 76r; see p.31). Sample cantucci, a crunchy Tuscan biscuit, and delve into the heritage of this 160 year-old bakery in the upstairs museum. Across the street, explore exquisite handmade silver cutlery at (5) **Pampaloni** and ask about their unique dining experience, **In Fabbrica** (see p.77), within their workshop.

12.30PM Cross Ponte Santa Trinita and turn right onto Via di Santo Spirito and head to (6) **Il Santino** (see p.47), a gastronomia in a cosy former wine cellar. Savour small plates of beef carpaccio, pecorino and pancetta crostini or terrina di fegatini di pollo (chicken liver pate) washed down with a dry, sparkling Prosecco from Veneto.

3PM Head away from the Arno down Via dei Serragli to (7) **Desinare** (at 234r), an incredible homewares store with a stellar kitchen section for the chef enthusiast. They host regular cooking, table design and food photography workshops. Backtrack to Via Santa Maria and turn left on Via delle Caldaie to become a pasta master at (8) **In Tavola** (Via dei Velluti 20r). Here you can prepare three types of homemade pasta and sauces to match the shapes (very important in Italian cooking) and dessert.

8PM If you can squeeze in more food, try a southern Italian-style pizza from nearby (9) **Gusta** (see p.192) and admire the neighbouring church of Santo Spirito. Follow with a sweet treat from (10) **Gelateria Della Passera** (see p.180), who hand-make their creamy creations.

FLORENCE FOR FASHIONISTAS

FULL DAY ITINERARY

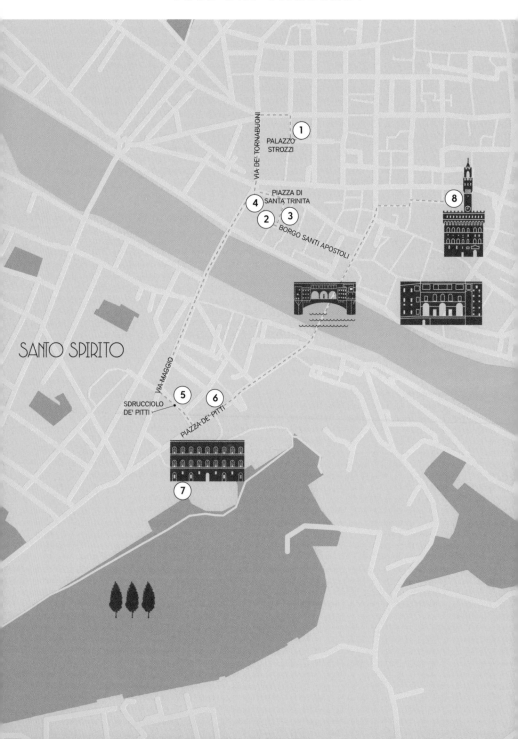

VIA DE' TORNABUONI

1 PALAZZO STROZZI

PIAZZA DI SANTA TRINITA

4

2 3

BORGO SANTI APOSTOLI

8

SANTO SPIRITO

VIA MAGGIO

SDRUCCIOLO DE' PITTI

5 6

PIAZZA DE' PITTI

7

Florence and fashion are intrinsically linked with high fashion houses like Gucci, Pucci and Ferragamo calling the city home. Take in the couture sights on both sides of the river Arno, visiting acclaimed shopping districts and learning about Florence's fashion history at the city's museums and galleries.

9AM Enjoy a late breakfast at ① **Strozzi Caffè** (see p.155), tucked within the courtyard of the 16th-century palazzo. Try a simple breakfast, Italian style, of espresso and a delicate pastry. Post breakfast, wander along the elegant Via de' Tornabuoni, peering into the showrooms of luxury labels of Armani, Gucci, Pucci and Prada.

10AM Veer left onto Borgo Santi Apostoli and swing by ② **Viajiyu** (see p.96) at number 45r for stylish women's shoes and their new men's collection. Grab the ideal accessory across the road at legendary Florentine designer ③ **Angela Caputi** (see p.123) at number 44-46r.

11AM Continue your shoe lust at ④ **Museo Salvatore Ferragamo** (see p.151) within stunning 13th-century Palazzo Spini Feroni on Piazza di Santa Trinita. The flagship store is here, as well as a museum depicting Salvatore Ferragamo's journey to Hollywood with a display of vintage shoes, some from the 1930s.

1PM Cross Ponte Santa Trinita and walk up Via Maggio with its mix of antique stores and new fashion outlets – perfect pre-lunch shopping. Turn left onto Sdrucciolo de' Pitti to find 'organic living room' ⑤ **Carduccio** (at 10r, see p.78) with its menu of raw food bowls, zoodles and cold-pressed juices. For more traditionally Tuscan fare, head to Piazza de' Pitti to ⑥ **Pitti Gola & Cantina** (see p.52), a contemporary wine bar in an antique book store.

3PM While away the afternoon at ⑦ **Museum of Costume and Fashion** (see p.165) within the southern wing of Palazzo Pitti. Take in the glamorous gowns and vintage accessories from the 18th century to present day, plus vintage garments from Chanel, Gucci, Versace and Prada.

5.30PM Heading back up Via de' Guicciardini, cross the famous Ponte Vecchio towards Piazza della Signoria (via Via Por Santa Maria and Via Calimaruzza). Finish your day the Gucci way, visiting their revamped museum, ⑧ **Gucci Garden** (see p.153), in a grand palace in Piazza della Signoria.

7.30PM After, take a seat in the lime green surrounds of **Gucci Osteria** (see p.63) also in Piazza della Signoria. The menu is by three-Michelin-star Italian chef Massimo Bottura. Choose between classic Italian cheesy tortellini pasta or opt for a more nouveau plate of deconstructed Caesar salad.

WINE

With a strong coffee culture focused within the city's traditional cafe bars, you can still sit in an old-world cafe, cappuccino in hand, and people-watch a morning away, or sip a classic espresso served under a frescoed ceiling. However, with Florence's many hip new cafes, now you can also enjoy a pour over in an industrial warehouse setting. Then there are Florence's incredible wine bars offering the finest selection of Tuscan and Italian labels, with passionate sommeliers who can pair your drink to your seasonal meal. From classic Chianti to new blends like Caberlot, this is a region with an exciting selection of bottles to sample and savour. Craft cocktails are also in demand and mixologists create innovative stiff drinks beyond the Spritz. From caffè until cocktail hour, WINE is a chapter of curated venues dedicated to a drink any time of day.

—

amblé

Vintage furniture with contemporary cocktails is a match made in Italian heaven.

With a 1950s feel of pre-loved furniture and a cocktail or two on offer, amblé is a treasure worth finding. Opened in 2013 by three friends, Barbara, Fabrizio and Lorenzo, amblé's philosophy is as simple as its strapline: Fresh Food and Old Furniture. Everything in the space is for sale – vintage armchairs, up-cycled beach loungers and bric-a-brac. Colourful vintage world maps cover the walls along with bold vintage letter signage.

Drink from antique china or crystal cups sourced locally and from antique markets in France and England. The amblé Spritz is worth trying: white wine, elderflower, lime, mint or a fresh juice made to order. In summer, deck chairs in its private courtyard are ideal for lounging. It's a bright, fun and friendly space to come with friends for lunch, an evening drink or to work, with free Wi-Fi.

Piazzetta dei Del Bene 7a

055 268 528

Tue–Sat
10am–10pm
Sun 12pm–10pm

€3–€7

W
www.amble.it

Caffé Gilli

Old world cafe and pastry shop in the centre of 'new' Florence.

Serving since 1733 and famed as Florence's oldest cafe, Gilli is an institution within the bustling Piazza della Repubblica. Gilli offers old world charisma with frothy cappuccini and stiff espresso served for standing patrons at a long marble-topped bar by dapper baristas in waistcoats and ties. For those wishing to linger, banquette seating within the elegant dining room has a *Room with a View* charm.

Begun as a Swiss pastry shop, Gilli's sweet treats are some of the finest in the city. Also a chocolatier, shelves are bursting with cocoa treats and colourful artisanal jellies. Lunch offers sandwiches and light bites and the best seats are by the open windows in the main cafe building overlooking the piazza.

Via Roma 1r

055 213 896

Daily
7.30am–12am

€1,40–€8

www.caffegilli.com

Wine

Antonio Mattei
Piccolo Museo Bottega

Celebrating the taste and history of Tuscan biscuits.

—

Once upon time I hosted wine tours in Tuscany taking small groups to incredible estates to delve into the practices of Italian winemaking. We would naturally sample the region's famed reds, sipping a glass while admiring the picture postcard landscape then finish with sweet wine, Vin Santo, paired with cantucci. These almond biscuits with a unique hard, crunchy texture are dipped into the amber liquor before eating, a typical way to end a meal, Tuscan-style. The biscuit's origins date back centuries with a long-standing heritage in the nearby town of Prato where bakers Antonio Mattei have been cooking these twice-baked creations since 1858. And now they have a piccolo museum and cafe in Florence where you can learn about, and taste, this sweet treat.

Piccolo Museo Bottega opened to celebrate Mattei's 160th anniversary, showcasing their long history as Biscottifici. The ground floor hosts a small shop selling colourful packets of biscuits, while freshly baked cakes are perfectly paired with a coffee in the museum's quaint, yet chic, cafe. Visitors can immerse themselves in the history of the biscuit business perusing memorabilia with work tools, photographs and antiquities on display, such as notable documents and packaging from the company's rich past.

Via Porta Rossa 76r

055 013 6203

Mon 3–7pm
Tue–Sun
10am–7pm

€3–€5

www.antoniomattei.com

Procacci

*A 19th-century salon
for the wine and truffle
aficionado.*

This truffle haven has been in situ on
elegant Via de' Tornabuoni since 1885
and continues to retain its 19th-century
salon feel. Founded by Leopoldo Procacci,
a passionate truffle connoisseur, the space
was recently refurbished yet retains the
original layout with L-shaped bar and wood
panelled walls filled with shelves of truffle
products — infused in butter, salt, olive
oil and jams. Wait staff move gracefully,
ready to pour your glass of choice (try the
sparking Rosé) from one of Florence's most
noble wine families, Antinori.

Choose from finger sandwiches layered in
truffle cream, anchovies and truffle butter,
or truffle with foie gras. Procacci also has a
gourmet shop, should you be so enamoured
by the truffle items that you wish to take
them home.

Via de' Tornabuoni 64r

055 211 656

Mon–Sat
10am–9pm
Sun 11am–8pm

€

€5–€8

www.procacci1885.it

Sei Divino

A passion for Tuscan wine and produce.

Tucked into the ground floor of a 14th-century pile, Palazzo Vespucci, Sei Divino is run by a young and enthusiastic sommelier, Neri Vignozzi, offering quality wines with over 200 labels and 100 styles to taste by the glass.

Sei Divino have proudly been sharing their passion for Tuscan wine and its food produce since 2003, with a food menu that changes daily offering dishes they call Aperigourmet. Quality is key with cheeses and cold cuts sourced from local Tuscan farms and fresh dishes made by their in-house chef, including favourite ceci (chickpea) pasta. Neri pairs all plates to a wine and will even customise a food/wine tasting just for you (book in advance).

Borgo Ognissanti 42r

Wed–Mon 6pm–1am

€
€5–€8

055 215 794

W
www.seidivinofirenze.it

Todo Modo

A boutique bookshop, cafe and event space in one,
ideal for the literary lover.

—

I've always been a lover of books and wanted to be surrounded by paper tomes, so Todo Modo is my kind of place. A boutique bookstore with a collection of 15,000 titles, new and used, in English and Italian, plus cards, wrapping paper and gifts. The main library room is tucked at the back of the store with tiered bench style seating ideal for lounging whilst perusing books, or watching regular events – performances, concerts, workshops and monthly spoken-word showcases.

Its in-house cafe, Uqbar, is named as a tribute to Argentinian author Jorge Luis Borges. Pop in for coffee and cake, all produce is purchased daily from local greengrocers and bakers. Or grab a glass of wine recommended by staff member Davide, an oenologist. In the cafe, you'll also find a selection of newspapers and magazines plus free Wi-Fi, making it a great stop while exploring Florence.

📍	🕐	€
Via dei Fossi 15r	Tues–Sat	€3–€5
	10am–8pm	
📞		W
055 239 9110		www.todomodo.org

Wine

La Ménagère

*From coffee to cocktails, flowers
and furniture included.*

—

Its name is a nod to the first homewares store in Florence which occupied this site from 1896, and today's version of La Ménagère is a cafe, restaurant, homewares store and in-house florist. With exposed walls, metal window finishings and lovely natural light, it creates a modern showroom nestled within the former coach house of 16th-century Palazzo Ginori, once home to the Florentine family famed for its porcelain business. Pull up a pew at the wood-panelled bench in the main bar for fresh coffee (supplied by Ditta Artigianale, see p.39) and be lured in by pastries and cakes in a glass cabinet. An open kitchen creates lunch plates with beef carpaccio, salad bowls like Lola (orange, fennel, anchovies and parsley pesto) and gourmet panini layered with ham, artichoke cream and salted ricotta.

In the restaurant sit under the flower installation or at the 18-metre long dining table where you can order from tasting menus or a la carte, choosing from dishes of ginger honey duck breast with citrus jam or green herb ravioli with lettuce foam and crunchy Culatello ham. Desserts include salted pastry with caramel cream, licorice and thyme. Post dinner, swing by the basement bar for craft cocktails and live jazz from Thursday until Sunday well into the late night hours (see p.203).

| 📍 Via de' Ginori 8r | 🕑 Daily 7.30am–2am | € €2–€8 |
| 📞 055 075 0600 | | W www.lamenagere.it |

Wine

Le Murate Caffè Letterario

Get your caffeine fix within the grounds of an old jail.

Set within the walls of a former convent built in 1424 for Benedictine nuns, Le Murate Caffè Letterario is today a peaceful and secluded space serving coffee and food within its quiet courtyard. In 1845, it was repurposed as a jail for male prisoners, remaining this way until 1985. You can still see the metal bars on windows of the newly revamped resident apartments, and former cell doors leading into modern office spaces.

Aperitivo buffet from 7pm is popular with students while a two-course 'smart lunch' is a go-to for local office workers at only €8. The sun-drenched courtyard is littered with vintage furniture and in summer, from a purpose built stage, live jazz, rock or classical music is performed. The complex is a cultural and recreational hub hosting art, film and poetry events.

Piazza delle Murate

055 234 6872

Mon–Fri
10.30am–1am
Sat–Sun
3pm–1am

€

€3–€7

W

www.lemurate.it

Ditta Artigianale

Coffee by day, gin by night, this cafe satisfies from dawn 'til dusk.

Step inside Francesco Sanapo's light and bright cafe and you're likely to be welcomed open-armed, literally – for he is a man with a big character. A Florentine, Francesco spent 15 years travelling to source the black bean, from Brazil to Guatemala and El Salvador. In 2013 he ranked 6th in the World Barista Championships in Australia, and Melbourne's laneway cafes inspired his vision for Ditta Artigianale. From simple espresso to three brewing methods, this is serious coffee made to match the Anglo brunch food.

Come night, gin cocktails are served using over 50 different labels including signature brand, Peter in Florence. The city now boasts outposts in hip Santo Spirito (Via dello Sprone 5r) and in art-house cinema, La Compagnia (Via Camillo Cavour, 50r).

Via dei Neri 32r

055 274 1541

Mon–Thurs
8am–10pm
Fri 8am–12am
Sat 9.30am–12am
Sun 9.30am–10pm

€

€3–€7

W

www.dittaartigianale.it

Libreria Brac

A tranquil modern oasis in the heart of old Florence.

—

Finding a quiet space to relax away from Florence's frenetic beat is a rarity, so hail Libreria Brac. A space that fuses cafe, restaurant and bookshop, its modern style is the antitheses of the aging yellow sandstone in the streets of Santa Croce. Tucked down an innocuous street, there is no sign above the door so finding it is part of the adventure.

The front section is cosy yet bright with a small bar, white wooden stools, and walls clad with Polaroid-style pictures of the vegetarian dishes on offer. From here you can see into the kitchen where hearty plates are prepared. Behind the bar, wait staff blend fruit smoothies or pour Italian wines, with deep reds to crisp dry whites like a fruity Carricante, Chardonnay and Albenello blend from Sicily. The inner courtyard is overtaken by an installation of draped mesh fabric floating above head level with armchairs and hidden nooks to nest while reading one of the magazines scattered on tables. Within the restaurant, bookshelves are filled with tomes dedicated to art, architecture, photography and design which you can browse or buy. Come nightfall, candles and soft lighting create a mood ripe for romance.

Via dei Vagellai 18	Mon–Sat 12pm–4pm, 7pm–12am	€3–€8
055 094 4877	Sun 7pm–12am	www.libreriabrac.net

Wine

Café 19.26

A little French fancy in Sant'Ambrogio.

The owners of Café 19.26, Matteo and Paola Del Re, admit to 'stealing' the atmosphere of Paris' Montmartre with its Art Deco inspired interior. Pop in, like a local, for an afternoon espresso or a sneaky Prosecco, and sip it in one of the library-like drawing rooms within the cafe's maze-like interior.

At lunch, the menu offers light bites of crostini, fresh pasta and a few French dishes. By nightfall a cocktail crowd arrives. There's 380 bottles on offer in a gentleman's club-style rum room with wood panelling, low light and stained-glass windows.

Via Giovan Battista
Niccolini 30r

055 234 6296

Mon–Fri
7am–1am
Sat 8am–1am

€

€1,50–€8

www.cafe1926firenze.com

Cibréo Caffé

Old world elegance in Sant'Ambrogio.

With wood panelled walls and red velvet seating, reminiscent of a 19th-century Viennese cafe, you know you're in for a comfortable stay. Sip a cappuccino and indulge in a light fluffy pastry as you watch the locals pass en route to Mercato di Sant'Ambrogio (see p.172). Eccentric owner, Florentine Fabio Picchi, often stops by with a bright 'buongiorno' to his clientele, a sign of the warmth you'll feel at Cibréo.

For lunch, meat-filled panini are popular (try their Tuscan Club sandwich layered with roast beef) and an aperitivo sipped from its streetside terrace is ideal come dusk. For dinner, a set menu starts from €40 per person. Alternatively, pop across the street to Cibréo Trattoria (Via de' Macci 122r), or a more refined dining experience at Cibréo Ristorante (Via Andrea del Verrocchio 8r).

Via Andrea del
Verrocchio 5r

Tue–Sun
8am–1am

€

€3–€8

W

www.cibreo.com

055 234 5853

Wine

Rasputin

*When Russia comes to town,
you know you'll be in good spirits.*

—

Named after the Russian mystic and self-proclaimed holy man assassinated in St Petersburg in 1916, this 'secret' bar has been a word-of-mouth hit since it quietly opened in 2016. There's no street number, just directions – you need to find the basement bar and ring a discreet doorbell nestled within a small alcove fashioned on a private chapel with church pew and crucifix hanging on the wall.

Established by Marco Vinci, Rasputin has a distinctly British gentleman's club-feel tucked under an exposed brick arch ceiling, warmed by walls in a blood-red hue and furnished with antiques and dimly lit lamps. Seasoned wait staff guide you through a drinks list that has a prohibition-era flair. Cocktails are stiff and perfectly blended created by head bartender Daniele Cancellara who revisits old classics using only the finest raw ingredients. Shelves behind the wood panelled bar house over 300 bottles of spirits (100 of which are whiskys) plus a selection of fine old-world wine from Italy and France, including Champagne, available by the bottle. With only 43 seats, reservations are wise and can be made until 11pm each night.

Borgo Tegolaio
(the number is a secret)

055 280 399

Sun–Thurs
8pm–2am
Fri–Sat
9pm–3am

€7–€9

W

www.facebook.com/rasputinfirenze

Wine

Il Santino

Hole-in-the-wall gastronomia for cosy wine moments.

—

In 2008, Il Santino's owners Stefano Sebastiani and Marco and Martina Baldesi wanted to create a Tuscan tapas bar – a brand-new concept in Florence. So they opened this gastronomia focusing on sourcing high quality produce and fine wine from small local producers. Housed in a former wine cellar, it's a cosy nook featuring exposed brick, wooden beams, shelves stacked with wine, and only four small tables and a collection of iron stools at the bar. In summer, patrons spill into the street enjoying the warm evenings.

Behind the central counter, cured meats hang from hooks, while beneath in a display cabinet there are marinated vegetables and cheeses from across Italy, France, England and Belgium. Savour small plates from pappa al pomodoro to cheesy truffle sausage crostini, washed down with a wine paired from an extensive list served by the glass or bottle. Il Santino is the sister space to the equally delectable Il Santo Bevitore (see p.75), two doors down.

Via di Santo Spirito 60r

Daily
12.30pm–11.00pm

€5–€8

W

055 230 2820

www.ilsantobevitore.com

Wine

Pint of View

Craft beers and cocktails with a Korean twist.

—

The team behind local brewery, Archea Brewery (on Via dei Serragli), wanted to create a place where they could linger when off duty. A place offering artisan beers and comfort food beyond classic Italian dishes. Twelve craft beers from Europe and beyond are on tap, with more by the bottle served from a long zinc bar. The interior has a gastro pub vibe with olive green banquettes and wooden tables under overhanging lamps.

The menu offers juicy burgers and the recent addition of Korean/Tuscan fused dishes by chef, Yejin Ha. Try the lampredotto mandu – a Korean dumpling stuffed with traditional Florentine-style tripe served with salsa verde. Cocktails, by bartender Lorenzo Pizzorno, are creative using in-house infusions with their take on the Spritz, the Pferffer, its pepper infused Aperol, Bitter Campari, sparkling wine, and orange soda a spicy version of the classic drink. Come Sunday for roasts and Bloody Marys and linger over dinner late into the night.

Borgo Tegolaio 17r

055 288 944

Mon–Wed
6pm–12am
Thurs 6pm–1am
Fri–Sat 6pm–2am
Sun 12pm–12am

€

€4–€8

www.pintofview.it

Wine

Le Volpi e l'Uva

*Fine wine and crostone to match keep regulars
returning for more.*

—

Tucked in a quiet piazzetta just a skip from Ponte Vecchio, Le Volpi e l'Uva (The Foxes and the Grapes) is a favourite with foodies and local wine enthusiasts who gather at the streetside tables to sample glasses of wine from local vineyards. Owners Ciro Beligni, Emilio Monechi and Riccardo Comparini opened its doors 25 years ago with a desire to showcase small wine producers from all over Italy, lovingly developing friendships with the makers and bringing their fruity finds back to the city. Be it by the glass or bottle, their selection includes Tuscan specific whites like Vernaccia di San Gimignano or a Vermentino from Sardinia. If bubbles is your tipple, try the sparkling wines from Veneto. Tuscan reds are represented en force from Chianti to Bolgheri and Montepulciano.

Famed for their succulent crostone bread slices layered with toppings, try the cheesy goodness of oozing Asiago with salty speck drizzled in honey, or grilled bread topped with meaty lard, the latter a delicacy in these parts, plus boards of cheeses, cured meats and breads from small specialty producers. Guided wine tasting can be arranged by appointment including a blind tasting session which features 8–10 samples, many organic and biodynamic.

Piazza dei Rossi 1r

Mon–Sat
11am–9pm

€5–€8

055 239 8132

www.levolpieluva.com

Wine

Pitti Gola & Cantina

Fine wine in an old bookstore make for a perfect pairing.

Wine and Florence go hand-in-hand and the team here serve up some of the best bottles in the city. Pop in to meet Shannon and Edoardo Fioravanti at this boutique wine bar housed in an old bookstore. It's incredibly intimate with just five tables tucked beside former bookshelves that display a fine collection of wine labels from Tuscany and Piedmont. The team focus on small, independent Italian wine producers with Edoardo, along with brother Zeno and business partner Manuele, on hand to share their sommelier expertise.

Offering wine tastings by the glass or bottle and a dining menu matched to wine pairings, it's the perfect wine stop. In summer, the outside tables offer picturesque Palazzo Pitti (see p.163) views. They also run Osteria dell'Enoteca (see p.81).

 Piazza de' Pitti 16

 Wed–Mon
12pm–11pm

 €5–€9

 055 212 704

 W
www.pittigolaecantina.com

Kawaii

Little Japan in Florence.

In their own words, a 'reinterpretation' of the classic sake bar/shop Izakaya, the Italian owners of Kawaii have created an intimate space with clean white lines and a long table adjoining the bar, ideal for a solo or date night out. The little sister to neighbouring Japanese restaurant, Momoyama, Kawaii is quintessential Japanese for a sake-inspired cocktail pre- or post-dinner.

With 30 types of sake on offer plus Japanese beer, whisky, gin and rum, bartenders have Asia-fied the cocktail classics with Sake Negroni (gin, Campari, vermouth, sake) or Tokyo Mule (vodka, ginger beer, sake). They also whip up small plates of Japanese dishes if you fancy a little sashimi paired with your sake.

Borgo San Frediano 8r

Tues–Sun
12.30pm–2.30pm,
6.30pm–1am

€

€6–€8

055 281 400

W

www.kawaiifirenze.it

Wine

Tasso Hostel

Music and cocktails in an old school hall? Yes, sir!

—

Within a converted secondary school, once run by nuns, Tasso is the vision of Romina Diaz and Lorenzo Bruzzichelli, a secret yet accessible venue full of surprise, wonder and fun. With a discreet entrance on a residential tree-lined street, once inside you are greeted with the grandeur of the old school hall, vintage furniture and a piano which takes centre stage for nightly music and open mic nights (see p.200).

Resident bartender Lorenzo is at your cocktail service mixing classic Spritz or creating something bespoke just for you. Upstairs you'll find a hostel with 13 bedrooms dressed in a minimal interior style. And with regular Sunday brunch, and markets in the courtyard during the warmer months, it's an escape from the heady buzz in the city centre and where you can enjoy a lively night out with locals.

Via Villani 15

Daily
7pm–1am

€6–€8

055 060 2087

www.tassohostelflorence.com

Wine

Mad Souls & Spirits

Their playful passion for cocktails is intoxicating.

—

I first met bar maestro Julian Biondi when he worked at a riverside cocktail bar during my early days in Florence. His passion for booze, in the best sense, was intoxicating (pun intended) and I've been following his bar hopping movements ever since. So when he teamed up with fellow mixologist, Neri Fantechi to open Mad Souls & Spirits I followed him over the Arno, like many of his loyal devotees.

From within a small and cosy bar room, beautifully created cocktails with quirky names are poured. Gin lovers rejoice in Un Rabbino Mi Disse (A Rabbi Told Me) based with London Dry Gin then topped with lemon juice, raspberry shrub syrup and bubbly Prosecco while Pane Burro & Marmellata (Bread Butter & Jam) combines classic rye whiskey with Campari infused butter and Vermouth laced orange jam. Shamelessly self-proclaimed 'awesome-est cocktail bar in Europe and Micronesia', you'll begin to understand their tongue-in-cheek playfulness that spills over into their drinks. Grab one and settle onto a stool in the al fresco terrazza as the sun goes down over the streets of San Frediano.

Borgo San
Frediano 36–38r

Daily
6pm–2am

€7–€9

W
facebook.com/madsoulsandspirits

055 627 1621

Wine

Santarosa Bistro

Greenhouse-style shack for drinks, jazz and yoga in the garden.

—

Finding a green space in the centre of Florence is a rarity, so when Santarosa Bistro opened in 2016 there was a collective sigh of green-tinged relief. Beside the medieval walls in the city's hip southern 'hood of San Frediano, you can sit inside its greenhouse-styled space surrounded by '50s furnishings, or perch outside on comfy cushions on recycled wooden crates as you sip on a coffee or Spritz.

Nights are jazzed up with live music in the garden, or start your day with a juice and try a daytime yoga class. Sundays see the space host a brunch buffet with DJs offering soothing weekend sounds. The bistro menu offers classic pasta dishes matched with a superb wine list curated by the team at Pitti Gola & Cantina (see p.52). Or opt for a seafood dish of mussels, or a veggie option like stuffed zucchini flowers, followed by a pot of pistachio tiramisu.

Lungarno di Santarosa

055 230 9057

Mon–Fri
8am–12am
Sat–Sun
10am–12am

€3–€7

W

facebook.com/santarosa.bistrot

DINE

Florence has seen an explosion of new dining venues in
recent years that balance seasonal Tuscan produce with
international flair, and give refined variety to the past weight
of traditionally heavy Tuscan cuisine. It's a delectable city for
the food enthusiast, and emphasis remains on locally sourced
food and wine, celebrating Tuscany and its neighbouring
regions. Dinner starts late and is to be lingered over, whether
you desire to dine in a leafy piazza, among olive groves,
or in a silversmith factory and savour the locally cured
salami, cheese and freshly hand-rolled pasta. My favourite
foodie escapes are within the walls of artisan shops (like In
Fabbrica, see p.77) or tackling a tripe sandwich at 9am
in Il Mercato Centrale (see p.67). Food, like travel, should
be adventurous and worthy of a little abandon. Within
this chapter of DINE, I take you to the best restaurants in
Florence to tantalise your tastebuds.

—

Gucci Osteria

Iconic fashion house serves up equally eclectic dishes.

—

Combine an iconic Italian fashion-house and famed three-Michelin-star Italian chef Massimo Bottura and you have Gucci Osteria, an elegant restaurant on the ground floor of Palazzo della Mercanzia which houses the Gucci Garden museum (see p.153). Having once again been awarded the grand title of World's Best Restaurant 2018 (for Osteria Francescana in Modena), Gucci Osteria Bottura creates a menu where iconic Italian dishes vie for attention with American 'classics'. A chianina hot dog and a deconstructed (layered) Caesar salad share the list with tortellini in creamy parmesan sauce, the latter a dish more representative of Bottura's Emilia-Romagna roots.

Relax into a green velvet banquette seat in the main dining room with walls splashed (to clash) in lime green, and admire shelves featuring ancient crests from the old palazzo facade. Crisp white linen covers tables, cushioning vintage designed ceramic plates and silverware, continuing Gucci's current eclectic styling from showroom to dining experience. Reservations are recommended.

Piazza della Signoria 10

Daily
12.30–3pm,
7.30–10pm

€15–€25

📞

055 7592 7038

W

www.gucci.com

Dine

Cantinetta Antinori

14th-century winemakers continuing Tuscan traditions.

The Antinori family has been winemakers in Tuscany since 1385. In this cosy restaurant on the ground floor of their grand city palace, dishes are cooked to traditional recipes, creating an old-world dining experience and attentive service.

The kitchen follows the rhythm and seasons of Tuscany, offering fresh pastas and game. In truffle season, buttery pasta with shavings of this prized root is to be savoured. When on the menu, try carciofi (artichoke) tagliatelle or a plate of porcini mushrooms hot off the grill. Maître d' Daniele happily suggests dishes, daily specials and which glass you should sample first from the family's 29 wine estates. All the Antinori wines are on offer, by the glass or bottle, from Chianti Classico to crisp Vermentino from Bolgheri.

Piazza degli Antinori 3

055 292 234

Tues–Sun
12–2.30pm,
7–10.30pm

€

€15–€25

W

www.cantinetta-antinori.com

Floret

Superfood surrounded by couture make for a fashionable pairing.

An oasis within the walls of high-end fashion store Luisa via Roma, Floret is a welcomed serene addition to inner city Florence dining. Away from the hustle of the shopping streets below, this courtyard cafe on the first floor of the fashion emporium is surrounded by leafy ferns in pots, with 1960s inspired decor in muted pastel shades and indoor sofa seating under a canopy ceiling.

The seasonal menu is good greenery too with superfood salad bowls, fresh sandwiches and pressed juices. Tuck into dishes like tabbouleh with grilled lemon chicken or a Dr Green smoothie (pineapple, spinach, banana, mint, avocado, wheatgrass, matcha), a meal in itself. With many gluten-free and vegan dishes, as well as non-dairy options – try the Golden Turmeric latte – its organic, clean eating will satisfy any fashionista or wellness seeker.

Via Roma 19-21r

055 295 924

Mon–Sat
10.30am–7.30pm
Sun 11am–7.30pm

€10–€14

W

www.floret-bar.com

Dine

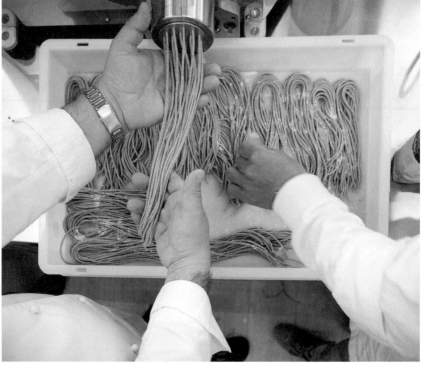

Il Mercato Centrale

*Fresh food, and fast, within Florence's
oldest running food market.*

—

In 2014 San Lorenzo's food emporium, Il Mercato Centrale, celebrated
its 140th birthday (having opened in 1874), with a refurbishment fit for
the seasoned foodie. Its sun-drenched upper floor glasshouse interior,
exposed iron metal beams and oversized wicker light fittings create a
bright, contemporary space with communal tables and food stalls offering
mouthwatering local tastes.

SUD creates perfect southern-style pizza with a chewy base and dripping in
creamy mozzarella, or sit at the galley bench at Tosca, a trattoria-style affair
to watch the chefs at work whipping up fresh pasta plates and meat dishes.
Franco Parola offers hundreds of creamy cheeses – try the silky burrata
that melts in your mouth. There is a mix of sweet and savoury, fresh or fried
dishes to delight any palate. If arriving before 2pm, peruse the downstairs
stalls selling produce to locals and neighbouring restaurants. Part of the fun
at this lower level is sampling olive oil, balsamic vinegar, pesto and wine as
you explore its food-infused corridors.

♀	◷	€
Piazza del Mercato	Daily	€6–€12
Centrale	8am–12am	
		W
☎		www.mercatocentrale.it
055 239 9798		

Braciere Malatesta

A family-run trattoria offering hearty Tuscan dishes.

The Baglioni family has been running this trattoria since 1954, their charcoal grill and wood-fire oven working tirelessly for decades. The menu is authentic Tuscan and seasonal, with bistecca, pasta and pizza en force. Recently refurbished, the interior has exposed walls, mix-matched '50s furniture and string lamps from the ceiling, offering a fresh yet vintage feel with utensils lining the walls becoming decorative 'art'.

For fresh pasta try Tuscan favourites like pappardelle with wild boar sauce or hand-rolled pici with sausage and black cabbage. Or for pizza, try the Fumaiola with its rich marinated pachino tomatoes, smoked burrata cheese and basil. In the warmer months the best seats are in the hidden garden, a tranquil oasis away from the frenetic pace outside in the streets of San Lorenzo.

Via Nazionale 36

Daily
12pm–11pm

€6–€12

055 215 164

W

www.bracieremalatesta.com

La Prosciutteria

Panini joint of choice within the bustle of Via dei Neri.

Past the endless number of sandwich shops on Via dei Neri, it's easy to miss my favourite establishment – a quirky hole-in-the-wall space. Under clusters of hanging prosciutti you enter a narrow room, with a long cabinet housing saucepans of fillings, fresh focaccia stacked in rows and rounds of pecorino cheese ready to be sliced. It specialises in made-to-order sandwiches and platters using a fine selection of meats, cheeses and vegetables.

Tables are repurposed from wooden wine boxes, lampshades fashioned from old tin cans and walls filled with artefacts from Tuscan days of old. The interior is a nod towards La Prosciutteria's heritage – all ingredients come via a sister company in Montespertoli just outside Florence, run by a line of farmers dating back 400 years.

Via dei Neri 54r

Daily
10.30am–11pm

€4–€7

055 265 4472

W
www.laprosciutteria.com

Dine

Arà: è SUD

*Be seduced by Sicilian cuisine cooked
to southern perfection.*

—

What started as a hole-in-the-wall snack stop near the Galleria dell'Accademia (see p.159) has grown into a full restaurant in a quiet backstreet in Santa Croce. With Sicilian roots, the menu at Arà: è SUD is a nod to the region's food heritage with classic dishes like Pasta alla Norma in all its intense tomato-and-eggplant-sauce glory (topped with grated salty hard ricotta) using handmade techniques and a regional flour. Chef Carmelo Pannocchietti, a Sicilian native, has been cooking since age seven. The son of bakers, his early career focused on creating sweet treats and fresh pasta, before opening his first restaurant three decades ago.

From Sicily's southern waters comes a fresh fish influence on the menu, plus dishes like Noccioline di Ara – a selection of mini arancini. For dolce, cannoli is done correctly – freshly piped to order with ricotta cream then dressed with finely chopped almonds and pistachios. The wine list focuses on Sicily with a little branch-out to other Italian regions. The interior is chic, simple yet slick, with a clean modern feel to the dining room. It's ideal for a group night out or an intimate dinner date.

📍
Via della Vigna Vecchia 4r

🕜
Wed–Mon 12pm–11pm

€
€8–€15

📞
331 217 0926

W
www.araristorante.it

Dine

PESCEPANE

STREET SEAFOOD

La Cucina di Pescepane

*Street food in a restaurant setting for lovers
of sensational seafood.*

—

Starting as street food served from a quaint Ape – a three-wheeled cart
transformed into a mobile kitchen – Pescepane found its popularity during
the summer months along the river Arno. Its fame grew so great its owners
opened a stand-alone restaurant in residential Sant'Ambrogio for all its loyal
fish followers to find. The interior has a water-based charm with lamps made
to look like lobster cages and blue walls creating a light and bright dining
room that seats just 25 people.

Tuscan summer salad panzanella 'del mare' is filled with juicy prawns and
soft calamari on a crunchy bread and cucumber base. Fish and chips fly out
of the kitchen as do fish burgers (try the 'black' version served in a charcoal
bun), plus there's a great selection of lightly battered calamari and prawns.
Save room for their cheese sandwich specialty – the 'mozzarella' with
anchovies, pecorino cheese, dried tomatoes, and herbs gently cooked to
golden perfection. A blackboard menu shows daily specials and, as it's just a
block from the local food market, expect only the freshest of ingredients.

Via Giosuè Carducci 15r

Tue–Sun
12pm–3pm,
7.30–10.30pm

€8–€15

055 234 4397

W

www.pescepane.it

Dine

Il Santo Bevitore

*Italian cuisine with a modern twist is
holier-than-thou.*

—

Il Santo Bevitore is one of those restaurants you keep returning to again and again. Opened by siblings Marco and Martina Baldesi, with childhood friend Stefano Sebastiani, they serve seasonal Italian produce with a twist on recipe tradition. The restaurant name translates as 'the holy drinker' and the interior decor is a testament to this, with bottles from 100 different wine labels, all sourced from small artisan producers across Italy, displayed on shelves above tables in the main dining hall. In the former coach house of a Renaissance palazzo, the restaurant shows no sign of its historic past. Instead, styling is simple yet elegant with white walls, dark wood tables and unpatterned china to create an ambience to suit a romantic dinner or a group ready for a foodie night out.

Head chef Pierluigi Campi creates dishes that change with the seasonal produce he sources: confit duck thigh with turnip blossoms and orange or soup of cauliflower foam with fried quinoa, capers and coffee. And then there is the wine ... deciding which grape to savour is half the fun with a fruity Syrah from Cortona, Il Castagno, a personal favourite.

Via di Santo Spirito 64r

Daily
12.30pm–2.30pm,
7.30–11.30pm

€10–€20

055 211 264

W

www.ilsantobevitore.com

Dine

In Fabbrica

*Dine amongst candelabras in
a silversmith workshop.*

—

By day it is the dining room to silversmith workshop, Pampaloni. Come nightfall In Fabbrica (which translates as 'in the factory') transforms into an intimate restaurant and opens its doors to the culinary curious. Hidden on a quiet residential street outside the medieval city gates, you first enter the downstairs showroom filled with glass cabinets showcasing the silverware. Next you make your way past the machinery and up a flight of stairs to the transformed canteen now sparkling under candlelight, the wait staff dressed in boiler suits. As silver is their business, tables are dressed in their finest creations, with grand candelabras, wine goblets and gleaming knives and forks. Soft downlights further create an air of romance and mystery.

The menu offers three plates in each course: starters, primi and mains. Dive into eggplant parmigiana or buffalo mozzarella ravioli with pistachios (in primi) with pork drunk in a citrus sauce for mains. A cover charge includes water, bread, dessert wine and coffee. Pampaloni's flagship store on Via Porta Rossa (at 99r) in Florence's city centre showcases In Fabbrica's silver creations, and cutlery and goblets can be purchased to take home to use for your own dining pleasure.

Via del Gelsomino 99	Wed–Sat 8–11pm	€12–€18
347 514 5468		http://restaurant.pampaloni.com

Dine

Carduccio

Dine in an organic living room for farm-to-table freshness.

Organic and biodynamic are movements in foodie cities including Florence, with a number of eateries proudly waving the 'green' flag. Owners Miranda and Filippo work with local farmers so the menu changes daily with what their vendors deliver. Carduccio's menu is farm-to-table, with raw food bowls, zoodles and cold-pressed juices. The 'organic living room' is a warm and inviting space with exposed brick walls, wooden tables, and natural materials.

Breakfast bowls are smoothie-style blends of banana, avocado or fruits topped with granola and seeds, while stiff Peruvian coffee in ceramic cups offers a morning caffeine fix. Lunch includes zesty soups (carrot and ginger is energising) with cakes and banana bread for dessert.

Sdrucciolo de' Pitti 10r

Mon–Sat
8am–7pm
Sun 10am–5pm

€8–€12

055 238 2070

www.carduccio.com

Gurdulù

Gentleman's club dining with a Tuscan twist.

Its dining room is slick and chic, with smoky grey walls, antique mirrors and paintings, flickering tea lights and banquettes in dark check fabric sitting bedside vintage wood tables. At the zinc bar, 'barlady' Cristina Bini offers a fresh look at cocktail mixing with names like 'Do You Remember Last Night?' and 'Speedy Gonzalez' (based in tequila). Begin your evening with a wine tasting (four glasses for €25), before the food love begins.

Chef Gabriele Andreon is a Florence native who has worked under Michelin-star maestros Mauro Colagreco and Heinz Beck. Andreon's menu is anything but traditional Tuscan – Marzolino cheese risotto with fava beans, vanilla and mushroom powder or duck breast with sweet kumquat, carrots and tart wasabi are two of my favourites.

Via delle Caldaie 12

Tues–Sat
7.30–11pm
Sun
12.3pm–2.30pm,
7.30–11pm

€12–€18

055 282 223

www.gurdulu.com

Dine

Osteria dell'Enoteca

Tuscan cuisine at its finest with a
Wine Wall to match.

—

If running one of the best wine bars in the city wasn't enough, the team from Pitti Gola & Cantina (see p.52) decided to open a restaurant specialising in bistecca and wine, the kind of place they would want to frequent on their day off. And you can see why. Opposite the walls of Boboli Gardens, (see p.184), the restaurant's exposed brick walls and linen draped tables offer a refined yet not-stuffy dining experience.

Chef Niccola Chiappi's menu is laced with seasonal local ingredients and four types of bistecca, from a house special to Chianina breed. Starters include creamy cheese zucchini flan (Flan di Zucchini con Crema di Formaggio), or paté aficionados will devour local specialty of fegatini (chicken liver) glazed with a sweet Vin Santo wine reduction. Then there are traditional crespelle (crepes) stuffed with ricotta cheese and spinach, or papero (goose) ragu tossed in fresh, thick, pici pasta. The team will happily perfect a pairing to suit your food from their hefty Wine Wall featuring Italian labels from small batches made by boutique wine producers.

Via Romana 70r

Wed–Mon
12pm–2.30pm,
7–10.30pm

€12–€25

055 2286018

W

www.osteriadellenoteca.com

Dine

SottArno

*The breakfast room of SoprArno Suites
is now open to all.*

—

SottArno is the breakfast room of boutique hotel SoprArno Suites (see p.207), serving its stayover guests before it opens its doors to the public from 10am. Offering a tantalising collection of specialty breads made from ancient grains as well as an array of sweet treats: breakfast cakes, crispbreads, cookies and the famous cantucci biscuits. Mortadella in rosemary bread is a speciality sandwich (and personal favourite), and salads are large and layered with ingredients such as tuna, egg and capers, a nod to a Nicoise.

Owner Matteo Perduca's collection of menus, gathered from dining experiences around the globe, adorn the walls while bric-a-brac furniture and banquette-style wall seating create a cosy atmosphere to sit and watch the Florentine world go by. This cafe is small enough to retain a serene charm in the middle of a bustling, vibrant city. Their well-priced cappuccino makes staying a while worth it.

Via Maggio 53r

Mon–Fri
10am–6.30pm

€6–€12

055 046 8719

W

www.fratellilunardi.it

Dine

Tamerò

Devour fresh pasta in an old mechanics workshop.

—

Handmade pasta isn't unusual in Florence, many of the city's finest eateries pride themselves on their fatti a mano (handmade) dishes. But what makes Tamerò memorable is its combination of contemporary decor with an adventurous pasta menu. Walk through the front door and gaze into the busy kitchen, where chef Gianmarco Desole makes fresh pasta – also available to take-away if you have access to a kitchen. Dive into plates of cheesy cacio e pepe pici or cacao-infused pappardelle tossed with wild boar. There's also a menu of creative plates showcasing a wide range of meats and fish. Save room for the dolce such as liquorice crème brulee with apple and caramello. For early-bird diners the Aperitivo buffet (see p.188) is a hearty mix of salads, pastas and hot dishes served from 6.30pm.

Occupying a building once home to a mechanic's workshop, Tamerò's interior retains much of the gritty feel of its previous guise with textured walls, exposed air-conditioning ducts, bespoke graffiti and shelves of books, along with rusty metal parts from the old car workshop hanging gracefully on the walls as art.

Piazza Santo Spirito 11r

055 282 596

Daily
12pm–3pm,
7pm–2am

€8–€15

W
www.tamero.it

Dine

L'OV

Veggie fare in a green-laced setting in fashionable San Frediano.

Vegetarian food has taken Florence by storm in a city renowned for meaty dishes, and with the opening of L'OV the plant-based dining options just became more exciting. In a greenhouse-style dining room, gluten-free and vegan options sit alongside a seasonal vegetarian menu. Try broccoli and bean burgers, chickpea patties on a bed of creamy coleslaw or crispy panzanella, a traditional Tuscan bread salad marinated in mandarin, artichokes, basil and spring onion. Having graduated from Istituto Alberghiero Saffi in Florence before travelling abroad as an apprentice, Chef Simone Bernacchioni takes inspiration from Puglia to classic Tuscan dishes, from South American street food to Japanese-inspired veggie sushi.

Enjoy a drink at the long bar covered in green moss before decamping to the bright red seating under a historic vaulted ceiling.

Piazza del Carmine 4r

055 205 2388

Mon 7–11pm
Tues–Sat
12pm–2.45pm, 7–11pm
Sun 12pm–3pm

€10–€15

W
www.osteriavegetariana.it

Burro & Acciughe

A little bit of Liguria in Florence.

Inspired by the Ligurian coast just north of Tuscany, famed for the villages of Cinque Terre, Burro & Acciughe's menu celebrates the sea. Fresh fish is displayed in a counter and walls are decorated with nostalgic seaside photos.

Crudi (raw) pieces of succulent red prawns or thinly sliced tuna come fresh from the counter, while antipasti of fried anchovies with sage or octopus salad with green salsa, are tasty starters. Anchovies are a feature – layered on buttered toast or tossed in fresh pastas. For mains, try lobster linguine or clams in orecchiette with fresh tuna and roasted eggplant. An extensive Italian wine list leans towards whites and sparkling varieties – sample the authentic Ligurian Terenzuola Cinque Terre DOC bianco. The team is always happy to pair the perfect wine to your sea catch.

Via dell'Orto 35r

055 045 7286

Tue–Sun
12pm–2pm,
7.30pm–12am

€8–€16

W

www.burroeacciughe.com

Dine

S.Forno

Fresh bread baked daily in an antique
Oltrarno oven.

—

For the past 40 years baker Angelo has arrived every morning to prepare fluffy treats for Florentines. One of the few remaining forno (bakeries) with original ovens on site (as opposed to baking outside the city centre and bringing in produce), behind an innocuous back door a massive steel oven is fired up at 4am daily. From 7.30am weekdays, S.Forno is open serving sourdough breads, baguettes and pizza slices while fresh panini is made to order, ideal for a quick lunch on the go. Fresh bread sits in wooden baskets behind the rustic wooden countertop while the smell of filtered coffee fills the air.

Local interior specialist Luca Rafanelli was recruited to bring his vintage furniture finds to match the distressed ceiling paintwork where lamps hang from long thin wires. Simple wood shelves offer fine produce to take home: jams, sauces, dry pasta, juices and artisan beer. Outside, below the 'Panificio' awning is a small chalkboard with a handwritten 'S.Forno', the only sign of the re-naming of this 100-year-old bakery.

Via Santa Monaca 3r

Mon–Fri
7.30am–7.30pm
Sat–Sun

€3–€6

055 239 8580

8am–7.30pm

www.ilsantobevitore.com

Dine

La Beppa Fioraia

A hidden garden oasis by the old walls of Florence.

—

It's easy to miss this tranquil green space by the medieval city walls in San Niccolò. Within a greenhouse-style shack, with coloured wooden chairs and windows on all sides, the dining room is a sun-drenched setting for lunch and lovely for dinner, anytime of the year. Named after a 19th-century Florentine, the wife of a Boboli gardener, who handed out flowers to local workers, it feels fitting in summer that you can dine amongst the olive grove in the restaurant's garden. It's a favourite spot to lose an afternoon with friends over a very long, and lazy, lunch.

Chef Leonardo Borghesi trained under Michelin-star chef Cristiano Tomei, and has created a modern menu with a Tuscan backbone. Well known for the sharing boards of local salamis, cheese and jams served with warm coccoli (salty fried bread dough) pasta also reigns: orecchiette (little ear-shaped pasta) is tossed with pappa al pomodoro, eggplant pesto and dry ricotta cheese; rabbit ragu is naturally salted with olives, capers and dill. At dinnertime, pizza aficionados will love the 48-hour stone-ground-flour bases. Choose from a classic like Quattro Formaggi or Beppa Fioraia layered with homemade pistachio pesto, tomatoes and stracciatella cheese.

📍 Via dell'Erta Canina 6r	🕗 Daily 12.30pm–2.30pm, 7.30–11pm	€ €7–€16
📞 055 234 7681		W www.labeppafioraia.it

Zeb

*Mother and son create perfect Tuscan tastes
in San Niccolò.*

—

One long table curves around a galley kitchen where freshly prepared food is served, while stools stand in a uniformed row from where you can see chefs at work through a gleaming glass window. The creation of Alberto Navari and his mother Giuseppina, Zeb is classic mamma's cooking at its finest with its menu based on family recipes. Zeb has been serving its flavourful plates since 2008, though the Navari family has occupied this space for over three decades. Initially it was a family run gastronomia, traditional delicatessen, before its conversion into its current guise – a sleek, modern dining space.

Dishes are listed on a simple blackboard menu, lovingly hand-written each morning by Alberto before being hung outside the restaurant entrance. Classic Italian recipes fill the menu with tagliatelle tossed with fresh tomatoes and basil or eggplant baked with gooey mozzarella. Daily specials are also exciting combinations – pear and ricotta ravioli in a creamy butter and poppy seed sauce, octopus potato salad, or Tuscan-herb-stuffed pork loin. As seating is limited with only 17 stools around the galley and four in the front window, arrive early to reserve your spot.

Via San Miniato 2r

Thurs–Tues
12pm–3.30pm
Thurs–Sat
7.30–10.30pm

€10–€15

055 234 2864

Dine

FINE

Florence and fashion have always gone together – since the Middle Ages when the city was a textile hub and leather-making centre. Florence's modern legacy is luxe designers like Ferragamo, Gucci and Pucci and today it's home to a vibrant scene of young designers with a desire for traditional craftsmanship with modern styling. Its shopping streets, like Via Maggio and Via della Spada, shouldn't be missed for independent stores, while you can't bypass a visit to the most chic of them all, Via de' Tornabuoni, where the high-end labels have flagship stores. If seeking quality leather, hand-bound books and paper, or jewellery, Florence's artisans give a contemporary touch to these traditional items with the Oltrarno neighbourhoods renowned for their studios. If travelling in January or July, enjoy the saldi (sales) when many items are 50% off. From clothing to perfume, jewellery and leather goods, FINE is a selection of independent stores to discover and buy directly from the makers.

—

Viajiyu

One-of-a-kind flats for the chic city traveller.

If you love to kick off your heels, then Viajiyu is your shoe lover's dream. Specialising in flats, for women and men, made in Italy and made to order, it's the epitome of slow fashion. Founder Nicole Still developed an appreciation for comfortable and fashionable shoes throughout her travels living and working on four continents, hence Viajiyu was born.

At their flagship store Viajiyu offers two options: a ready-to-wear collection or you can design your perfect shoe by choosing the material, trim and shape, and shoes will be shipped to your door within six weeks. With 25 styles to choose from including wedges, sandals and booties, shoes are made using only the highest grade leather and textiles from the best tanneries in Italy. Private shoe fittings are available, with appointments booked online.

Borgo Santi Apostoli 45r

Daily
10.30am–7.30pm

€

expensive

055 290 380

W

www.viajiyu.com

Boutique Nadine

New fashion with vintage accessories for curious clientele.

On a scenic street facing the Arno with views of Ponte Vecchio, Boutique Nadine is a Narnia-inspired wonderland of new and vintage fashion for men and women, jewellery and homewares. From old clothing trunks and wooden tables to retro chairs, there are many pieces perfect as unusual gifts. Then there's the tantalising Italian clothing including vintage Roberta di Camerino and Emilio Pucci, French houses of Chanel, Dior, Hermes and YSL, and emerging fashion designers sourced by owners Irene Zarrilli and Matteo Querini on their travels throughout Europe.

The boutique also includes their own labels: Irene adds her feminine flair with dresses by label, Odette, while Matteo, inspired by his Tuscan country retreat, focuses on men's cotton and linen shirts and wool jackets under the label, Vigliano.

Lungarno Acciaiuoli 22r

055 28 78 51

Mon
2.30–7.30pm
Tue–Sat
10am–7.30pm
Sun 12–7pm

€
inexpensive

W
www.boutiquenadine.com

Digerolamo

Heavenly handbags that are distinctly Florentine.

—

Both Clara Soto's grandfathers were shoemakers and they inspired her as a child to dream of making leather bags. Growing up in Ecuador and Argentina, young Clara would watch her grandfathers drawing patterns, creating shoe samples or handcrafting leather wallets. Digerolamo is a nod to her Italian roots as both sets of her great-grandparents came from the southern region of Basilicata, leaving Italy after World War Two. Moving to Paris in her 20s, Clara worked in jewellery design, yet her passion for leather remained. She discovered a course at the Scuola Del Cuoio (see p.109), and her future in Florence making handbags was secured.

The architecture, shapes and colours of worldly trips inspire Clara's designs, as do the colours of Florence: dusty terracotta, Chianti red and sandstone cremes, seen in the leather colours she sources. In her showroom, handmade creations are displayed, with every part of the product made in her basement workshop. Clara's handbags' intricate patterns are made using a handheld punch, she glues and stitches, and will even emboss your initials for an added artisan touch. The showroom also features contemporary jewellery created by her Argentinian-based mother who works with bronze to shape the pieces before being plated in 24-carat gold.

📍	🕐	€
Via del Moro 58r	Mon–Sat	expensive
	10am–1pm,	
📞	3–8pm	W
055 229 8378		www.shopdigerolamo.it

Fine

Marie Antoinette

Second-hand designer and vintage fashion to swoon over.

If you are looking to buy seriously stylish second-hand fashion, you'll discover rows of clothing from big design houses at Marie Antoinette, including Valentino, YSL, Chanel, Balenciaga, Prada, Louis Vuitton and Bulgari. Established by two former stylists, Geraldine Naldini and Cinzia Cioni, the ladies have been selling used, 'but not abused', as they say, items since 2014. As clothing is on consignment, stock is ever changing, making for that unique find. Having moved from their previous space in Piazzetta del Bene, their new digs sit on lively Via della Spada, a street that has become a go-to for shopping in recent years.

The accessories are as enticing as the clothing, with jewellery, shoes and handbags. This is a well-curated store with rare pieces for the fashion lover.

Via della Spada 38r

055 280 906

Tue–Sat
11am–7.30pm
Sun–Mon
2–7.30pm

€

moderate

www.marie
antoinettefirenze.com

Baby Bottega

A playful boutique for little people.

As a mother of four, Daisy Diaz knows a thing or two about keeping children happy. She brings a passion for family and design together at Baby Bottega, focusing on children's interiors, toys, games and clothing. Sourced from independent makers of gifts and goods she offers handmade products and designs for little people.

From vibrant wallpaper from Parisian atelier Bien Tait, handmade cushions and bedroom accessories via England's Little Cloud to newborn clothing by Californian brand Milkbarn, there are items to create the perfect playroom or playtime. Daisy also offers a calendar of events for families including storytelling laboratories, baking or flower arranging for children, etiquette lessons and regular one-off special events.

Via Il Prato 53–55r

Mon–Sat
10am–1pm,
2.30–7.30pm

inexpensive

055 286 091

www.babybottega.com

Fine

Benheart

Leather made with true love by a Florence-based designer.

If you are looking for that quintessential Florentine fashion item – a leather jacket – look no further than Benheart. It also sells beautiful handbags and accessories, unlike any you'll find in other leather stores or markets in Florence. Having previously been a leather designer for almost a decade, a near-death experience at age 29 made Ben vow to follow his dream to open a leather emporium, which he did with childhood friend Matteo in 2011.

Nappa leather is used to construct oversized slouchy handbags, and woven design patterns feature on moccasin shoes and ankle-length boots for men and women. Belts and accessories are ready-to-wear yet can be personalised with your initials. Should you desire custom-made, the duo can make pieces to order then ship anywhere in the world.

Via della Vigna Nuova 97r

Mon–Sat
9am–8pm
Sun 10am–8pm

moderate

055 239 9483

www.benheart.it

La Serra
M.K.Textile
Atelier

*Contemporary textiles
created in a classic
Florentine greenhouse.*

Florence's art and design remains steeped in artisan traditions using quality textiles, and La Serra M.K. Textile Atelier continues to lead this charge. Housed in a greenhouse within the tranquil private gardens of Palazzo Pandolfini, you will find textile designers Margherita Pandolfini and Karl Jorns, hand-painting or screenprinting original designs soon to become table runners, tote bags or fabric used to up-cycle vintage chairs. Margherita's work is constantly inspired by Florence, in her words: 'there is always something new or unexpected to discover when walking around the city'.

A visit to their studio is a unique Florence experience and can easily be made by appointment. Their prints are bold and modern using the highest quality fabric and pigments. Their products are ideal to dress your home.

Via Salvestrina 1

By appointment

inexpensive

349 580 3147

W
www.mktextileatelier.com

l'ora dell'amore
vita è il più bel

art925 by Naomi Muirhead

See inside a jewellery studio within a former convent.

—

Housed in a former convent tucked away from a busy San Lorenzo street, the art925 jewellery studio of Naomi Muirhead is alluring to find. Press the buzzer to step inside this secluded courtyard and see Naomi at work. Not a traditional store as it's a working school and craft studio, visits can be made by appointment to peruse her unique designs. With degrees in painting, interior architecture, and jewellery art it was a love for the 'intimate nature', as she calls it, of creating jewellery by hand that won her over to focus her creative talents on making one-off pieces with the city and its landmarks as her muse.

Many of her pieces have an antiquities feel, taking inspiration from the architecture of Italian churches and castles. Other ranges see old maps used in pendants or necklaces made using antique watch parts. Naomi's 'Text' range of jewellery, rings and necklaces have been created using paper from vintage books and old dictionaries, taking Italian words or phrases to be repurposed and set in sterling silver, making each piece utterly unique. You can also find a selection of Naomi's work at MIO Concept Store (Via della Spada 34r).

Via Guelfa 85

By appointment

moderate

328 229 6601

W
www.art925.com

Fine

Florence Factory

*Showcasing Florence's artisan heritage and a love
for modern design.*

—

What started life as a pop-up shop is now a stand-alone store in Santa
Croce dedicated to stylish products by Tuscan or Italian designers and
contemporary artisans of fashion, accessories, and ceramics. Creative duo
Jacopo Lotti and Lorenzo Bertini select emerging talent that represents 'new'
Florence, offering traditional craftsmanship with a modern design twist.

This store is filled with lust-worthy items, many created within nearby
workshops. There's jewellery from Officine Nora (see p.129), the fruity prints
of local fashion label Bastah Firenze, ceramics by Jaquelin Harberink, and
leather handbags by Majo. Thirty local designers specialising in handmade
crafts are featured, with the buying team focused on authentic regional
products. As many pieces are limited, there is no mass production on sale,
rather ideal take-home pieces uniquely from Florence.

Via dei Neri 6–8r

055 205 2952

Tue–Sat
10.30am–7.30pm
Sun–Mon
1.30–7.30pm

inexpensive

W

www.florencefactory.it

Fine

Scuola Del Cuoio

Historic Santa Croce leather school and shop for classic craftsmanship.

—

I first heard about Scuola Del Cuoio by word of mouth – had I been to the leather school and shop within the church grounds of Santa Croce? From the first time I entered, taking the discreet archway to the left of the church facade, I was mesmerised. The Gori family has been Florentine leather-makers for almost 100 years. In 1950, Marcello Gori was invited by the Franciscan Friars of Santa Croce to teach the skills of leather-making to World War Two orphans. The school is now housed in the former dormitory of trainee friars and continues to be a family affair. Sisters Laura, Francesca and Barbara Gori carry on the ethos of the school developed by their father.

The school is filled with students keen to learn traditional leather-making techniques with short half-day workshops to longer six-month courses available. Free weekday tours include a leather-making demonstration and longer technical visits (€14 per hour). For the shopper, tailored jackets, leather-bound notebooks, purses, bookmarks and bracelets are on sale from a showroom under magnificent 15th-century arched ceilings complete with Renaissance frescoes and the Medici coat of arms.

Via San Giuseppe 5r

055 244 533

Spring/Summer
Daily 10am–6pm
Autumn/Winter
Mon–Fri 10am–6pm,
Sat 10.30am–6pm

€

inexpensive

www.scuoladelcuoio.com

Fine

Aqua Flor

Sensuous scents for the sophisticated shopper.

—

One of the reasons I love Florence is the array of backstreets to explore, palazzo courtyards to enter and shops such as Aqua Flor that draw you in with a sense of intrigue. Aqua Flor is a perfumery full of scent-ual products crafted with passion. Created by perfume master Sileno Cheloni, the store is set in a 16th-century palazzo and harks back to a bygone era. Three rooms occupy the ground floor beneath glorious arched ceilings, walls lined with large wooden cabinets contain rows of brown glass bottles filled with botanical ingredients, while orange light shades add a warm ambience to these rooms that weave around a discreet inner courtyard.

Inspired by traditions of botanic extraction from the Renaissance, Sileno started his perfumery in Lucca before moving to Florence in 2011. Time in Milan working in essences and aromas and regular trips to Cairo were fundamental in forming Aqua Flor's philosophy — not to be a commercial industry, rather to use rare and sophisticated materials to create a small batch of scents. Over 1500 ingredients are used to create such bottled perfection in a basement laboratory where new 'nose' Nicola Bianchi also develops bespoke perfumes for clients should you desire a truly unique scent. Beyond perfumes, there are colognes, soaps, creams, candles and fragrant salts.

Borgo Santa Croce 6	Daily 10am–1pm, 2–8pm	inexpensive
055 234 3471		www.aquaflor.it

Fine

EleoLab

Exquisite headpieces to suit any ensemble.

—

Eleonora Marchi's passion for accessories finds her designing, drawing, and sewing all the headpieces, from hairclips to fascinator hats, that you see in her beautiful bottega. Each piece is handmade, including every flower petal, delicately created with fine materials using traditional techniques and antique work tools.

Having initially studied Culture and Stylist Fashion, Eleonora became intrigued by bespoke headpieces after learning from two elderly craftswomen who taught her the art of fabric flowers and became her Florentine mentors. Inside her workspace-cum-store, there's rows of headwear for women, many pieces inspired by nature, all handcrafted in fine silk, organza, satin, velvet or cotton. Eleonora also creates handbags, scarfs and brooches using the same handcrafted techniques.

Via Arnolfo 11r

Mon–Fri
10am–1.30pm,
3.30–7.30pm

inexpensive

347 551 5759

W
www.eleolab.it

Fine

Mimi Furaha

*Emerging designers of fashion and jewellery within
an antique palazzo.*

—

From a childhood spent in Africa, storeowner Michelle Brichieri Colombi
brings her passion for vibrant fashion to the tailored women's clothing at
Mimi Furaha, and garments are designed and made in Italy. The store's name
translates to 'I'm happy' in Kiswahili, with the showroom a bright and airy
space weaving through two large spaces on the ground floor of imposing
Palazzo degli Alessandri.

Brands featured are emerging designers with modern, contemporary style.
From the three-toned panelling of Pier Antonio Gaspari's wide-legged pants,
to shift dresses by Bastah Firenze, or '50s style knee-skimming skirts by Niù.
Handmade jewellery includes chunky necklaces by Magma Lab. Michelle,
along with business partner Raffaela D'Elia, also uses the store for events
and exhibitions to bring like-minded creatives together.

Borgo degli Albizi 35r

Daily
10.30am–12.30pm,
1.30–7pm

moderate

055 234 4456

W

www.mimifuraha.it

Fine

Sbigoli Terrecotte

Handmade ceramic creations since 1857.

—

This ceramics workshop and showroom, just a few minutes' walk from the Duomo, is a family-run affair; the Sbigoli family began the business as artisans in 1857 and since the 1920s the ceramics mantle has been handed to the Adamis who handle every aspect of production today. Antonella Adami, who in her eighties is still free-hand painting these delicate pieces, runs the store with daughters Chiara and Lorenza.

Hundreds of handmade tableware pieces grace shelves all lovingly hand painted in a small rear studio and fired within an onsite kiln. Plates, bowls, oil and vinegar sets, salt and pepper shakers, coffee cups and vases vie for shelf space, and are part of various collections: 'Autumn' is decorated with pears, grapes and plums wrapped in bright green leaves and a geometric pattern; 'Toscana' showcases the Tuscan countryside, its hills, olive groves, vineyards and cypresses trees. Designs are inspired by traditional Florentine art and Tuscan majolica methods – a tin-glazed pottery technique dating back to the Renaissance. They also offer short ceramic workshops and guided behind-the-scenes tours in English.

Via Sant'Egidio 4r	Mon–Sat	inexpensive
	9am–1pm, 2.30–7.30pm	W
055 247 9713		www.sbigoliterrecotte.it

Fine

Société Anonyme

Chic European styling to suit all styles and budgets.

Massimiliano Giannelli's eclectic showroom of international labels is a store that could easily be found in Berlin or the East End of London. With womenswear and menswear from Topshop to Kenzo, Maison Martin Margiela to Comme des Garçons, there is something for all styles and budgets. Massimiliano's passion for fashion has seen him also create an eponymous label inspired by Japan and Belgium, with clean cuts and loose-fitting shapes.

The store's interior has an industrial feel – clean, sparse and white with lots of natural light. Concrete floors, metal clothing racks full of garments, neon sign lights and untreated wood walls give an airy ambience. A second store has launched over the Arno (Société Anonyme Deux; Via Maggio 60r).

Via Giovan Battista
Niccolini 3f

055 386 0084

Mon
3.30–7.30pm
Tue–Sat
10am–7.30pm

€

moderate

W

www.societeanonyme.it

Bjørk

Constructed garments and designer reads for fashion-forward shoppers.

Tucked down a side street near Ponte Vecchio, Bjørk is an alternative fashion space featuring contemporary, leading-edge labels, for men and women, from Australia, Belgium, Denmark and Italy. It also has arguably the best and broadest collection of lifestyle books and magazines in Florence. Clothing is Nordic-inspired with constructed, clean lines made with rich textiles in muted tones, and shoes made in Tuscany from quality custom Italian leather. The rows of designer reads are mostly in English, and also cover fashion and photography.

A Florentine by birth, owner Filippo Anzalone opened the store in 2013 to challenge traditional Italian style beliefs while indulging in his passion for fashion. Living in London for three years working in art direction inspired his store's forward-thinking approach.

Via dello Sprone 25r

333 979 5839

Mon
2.30–7.30pm
Tue–Sat
10.30am–1.30pm,
2.30–7.30pm

moderate

Fine

Giulia Materia

Retro flair in notebooks, clothing and accessories.

Like many of the stores in the artisan neighbourhood of Santo Spirito, craftsmanship here is key. Designer Giulia Materia hails from Arezzo, studied at Bauhaus-Universtät Weimar, Germany, and was trained in binding at the Santa Reparata International School of Art in Florence. With partner Enzo Sarcinelli, she opened her shop and laboratory in 2012. Here, you'll find the duo behind their shop counter most days gluing together their latest notebooks ready for display.

Products in her snug store have a distinctly retro flair using bright, bold materials in block neon colours, stripes and prints. Overnight and gym bags and pencil cases are sewn with '70s inspired wool upholstery fabrics, notebooks are bound in bright cotton, and there's rows of shift dresses and coloured T-shirts to peruse.

Sdrucciolo de' Pitti 13r

Tue–Sun
10am–7pm

inexpensive

055 975 3975

www.giuliamateria.com

Anita Russo

Contemporary ceramics to brighten up any home.

Anita Russo came to Florence to study fine art before spending a year in Montelupo, a small town famed for its ceramics, where she learnt traditional clay techniques. Her ceramics studio and shop in Florence offers modern pieces in her signature bold style. Wine stoppers, vases, cups, plates and lamps are all displayed on shelves made from reclaimed ladders.

Her use of, and play with, colour is her trademark – most designs use a two-tone dipping technique and have a harmony between hues. Anita has a handmade philosophy – all pieces are created and fired within her studio in a kiln at the back of the store. She also runs short courses should you wish to create your own ceramic piece for a unique souvenir.

Via Romana 11r

Mon–Sat
11am–7.30pm

inexpensive

347 645 7047

Fine

Angela Caputi

Statement jewellery from a legendary
Florentine designer.

—

Walking into Angela Caputi's flagship store in Santo Spirito is captivating and not just because of the jewellery on display – it's also the experience. Established in 1975, Ms. Caputi began making jewellery inspired by the glamour of 1940s Hollywood films. She has a passion for elegant yet modern design and is one of the most recognised names in high fashion costume jewellery in Italy. Her pieces have featured in fashion exhibitions both in Florence and at New York's Museum at FIT and The Met.

Each piece is playful and sophisticated in style, woven by hand in the company's Oltrarno workshop using locally produced and colourful resin. Past collections have seen inspiration come from the ocean to Africa, and even earrings featuring Michelangelo's *David*. In-store, pristine white drawers display these stunning pieces of bejewelled art resting in black velvet trays. Half the fun of shopping here is exploring each drawer to see what pieces you'll discover. There is a second shop on Borgo Santi Apostoli (at 44-46r) that also sells handbags and clothing.

Via Santo Spirito 58r

Tues–Sat
10am–1pm,

moderate

055 212 972

3.30–7.30pm

www.angelacaputi.com

Fine

SARA AMRHEIN
CONTEMPORARY JEWELRY

Sara Amrhein

Bold statement jewellery to brighten up any outfit.

—

The colours of Sara Amrhein's bold handmade necklaces, bracelets, earrings and brooches are inspired by the vibrancy of sun-drenched Los Angeles, while the detail, intricate design and craftsmanship reflect her experiences of living in Florence, finding inspiration down every cobbled lane and bustling piazza. Sara also cites her fashionista aunt and mother, and artists such as Frida Khalo and Italian designers Dolce & Gabbana, as muses.

Her studio and showroom is a bright, light space with crisp white counters offsetting her coloured creations, just a skip from the hidden, yet charming, Piazza della Passera. Here you will find Sara at her worktable, kneading polymer clay, cutting it into original designs and assembling beading to create her final pieces. Flowers feature heavily with each petal lovingly molded by hand in bold block colours including pink, blue and bright yellow.

Via dello Sprone 9–11r

Wed–Mon
11am–7.30pm

€
inexpensive

392 961 3197

W
www.sara-amrhein.com

Fine

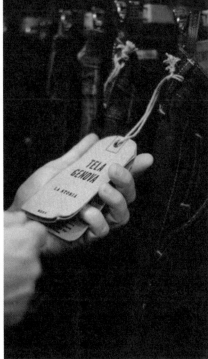

Dexter

Dapper Italian style by the river Arno.

—

The minute you meet Marco Meacci you know what's in store at Dexter. Incredibly dapper, in equal parts smart and stylish, the fitted waistcoat and tailored jeans are a preview of what's on the shelves within his boutique. Here, rows of Italian-made clothing for men and women take on a vintage twist with a design nod towards the 1940s and 1950s. Denim from Le Marche, shirts from Milan, dresses from Rome, jewellery created by local Florentine artisans, waistcoats and felt hats fill the cosy store.

With an international background in fashion, Marco began his career at Oliver in 1980, the go-to clothing store in Florence at the time, before heading abroad to the USA and Japan. After years of working for others, Marco decided to 'open my own little boutique' in 2009. Jazz saxophonist Dexter Gordon inspired the store's name, a musician of the bebop era and arguably the ideal musical accompaniment to the clothing hanging on Dexter's shelves: classic, stylish and a little smooth.

Via Maggio 7r

Daily
10am–1pm,
3.30–7.30pm

moderate

055 287 516

Fine

Tiziana Alemanni

Creative couture clothing with Sicilian shimmer.

Tiziana's stylish pieces are unsurpassed – from 1950s Audrey Hepburn-inspired dresses to '70s style wide-legged trousers – all hand-sewn onsite in her Oltrarno bottega by Palazzo Pitti. A Sicilian transplanted to Florence, Tiziana's southern warmth is as inviting as her designs, all made with sumptuous textiles rich in the feel of true Italian quality. 'I express myself through the fabric, it is my muse,' Tiziana says.

Inspiration from her home-island – its azure blue seas, bright sun hues and Baroque architectural styles – adds a classic feel to her contemporary pieces. Ready-to-wear items can be bought off the rack while bespoke tailoring is Tiziana's specialty – garments can be created within three fittings and then shipped, when ready, anywhere in the world.

Sdrucciolo de' Pitti 20

055 213 372

Mon 1–7pm
Tues–Sat
10am–7pm

expensive

www.tizianaalemanni.it

Officine Nora

Ring the bell to enter this modern jewellery studio and store.

Officine Nora encourages drop-ins so ring the bell and enter a modern bottega set in a former mechanics workshop, where a group of jewellery artists share the space yet work independently. Run by Margherita de Martino Norante, she works with five other designers who hail from Italy, Japan, Slovenia and the USA. Here you'll find contemporary pieces that are unusual and exclusive and all available to purchase.

If you're keen to dabble in design yourself, there are workshops from one-and-a-half hours to longer sessions such as 'Goldsmith for the day' over four hours, and all taught in English. Grab a workstation and use the onsite equipment including rolling mills, a hand-casting station, wax injector, enamel oven, micro flame, sanding machine and buckets of tools to create your very own necklace pendant.

Via dei Preti 2-4r

055 975 8930

Mon–Fri
11am–1pm,
3.30–7.30pm

moderate

www.officinenora.it

Fine

iVisionari

Fashion-forward eyewear in an old stationery store.

The words 'R. Cappelli Cartoleria' remain above the door, the facade of the former stationery store reminiscent of pre-war times, yet its interior is full of new eyewear in colourful shapes and sizes. Siblings Elena and Emiliano Lenzi have a shared passion for a unique eye experience: Elena, an eye specialist for almost three decades, tests eyes and helps you find the perfect frames, while Emilano sources new eyewear brands.

The interior style of the old shop is unchanged: original shelving restored in baby blue, the long countertop unmoved since the 1940s, while the windows display new products that are inviting and curious from boutique designers from Australia, France, Germany and Russia. Eye tests can be done within 30 minutes and glasses ready to take home the same day.

Piazza Nazario Sauro 14r

055 282 714

Tues–Sat
10am–1pm,
2.30–7.30pm

moderate

www.ivisionari.com

Coexist

Music, fashion, and events under one warehouse-style roof.

Coexist is a fashion hub and event space, housing local and international fashion labels, magazines and music. Run by a group of five creatives, they work with local artisans to create bespoke ranges for the store, proudly supporting local emerging talent. Their own eponymous clothing label, by two young Italian designers, Gem Marras and Eva Di Franco, reflects a minimalist look – modern, clean lines in black, whites and greys – for men and women, with some unisex pieces.

The store's interior has an industrial feel: distressed walls, warehouse panelled windows and rust-brown metal square shelves for hanging garments. A sneaky pulley system opens up the showroom and turns it into an event space for fashion shows and workshops, including visual merchandising for students from local fashion schools.

 Piazza Nazario Sauro 22r

 Mon 3.30–7.30pm
Tues–Sat
10.30am–7.30pm

€ moderate

 055 265 7515

 W
www.coexistore.com

Fine

Jane Harman

Bespoke wood products and jewellery with a local Florence flair.

Jane Harman's quaint store adjoins her south-of-the-river workshop selling her handmade pieces, all made of wood, from jewellery to candleholders, letters and numbers, penholders, and even mini versions of monuments, such as the local church of Santo Spirito. British-born Jane is an antiques restorer by trade with more than 30 years' experience in furniture and interiors. Originally venturing to Florence to train in traditional Florentine craft carpentry, today she also creates affordable chunky wood rings with neon-coloured touches or letters made into hanging necklaces (when she's not restoring historic palaces).

Jane is also an accomplished drawer, and you'll find original artwork of Florence's iconic buildings, made with ink, watercolour, charcoal and even walnut stain, sold as greeting cards. A beautiful take home of your trip.

Via Lorenzo Bartolini 1r

329 070 4920

Mon–Fri
8am–12.30pm,
2–6pm

inexpensive

www.harmanjane.it

Ink-P

Eye-popping colour and graphics for striking street style.

When you enter Ink-P you are overcome by the racks of bright neons, pinks and azure blues designed in the label's signature style. Creative team Giulia Castagnoli and Antonio Fugazzotto screenprint fabrics, including leather, in their workshop, that is then made into T-shirts, sunglasses, bags and shoes, all with their trademark striped yet floating designs. With mens- and womenswear plus a small range for children, every item is hand-printed then sewn, so each piece is one-of-a-kind.

Giulia and Antonio met at a creative agency and shared a dream for a life beyond office walls. During a year of travel their love for nature was reawakened. Nature's textures, patterns, animals, plants, hues, shapes, and colour have shaped their ethical approach.

Via di Camaldoli 18r

Mon–Sat
4–7.30pm

€

inexpensive

338 153 1560

W

www.ink-p.com

Fine

Hello Wonderful!

Sparkle in original designs by two local couturiers.

—

Young Italian designers, friends and fellow fashionistas Livia Quaresmini and Vivian Ventroni sketch, cut and sew every piece you'll find in their small boutique by Piazza del Carmine. The duo has a passion to create stylish womenswear with a social conscience. Much of their items are environmentally friendly using left-over materials from larger fashion houses to create '60s and '70s inspired ready-to-wear pieces. Everything you see here is wholly original, ensuring you a take-home piece that you won't see anyone else wearing.

Within a light and bright interior with a slick Nordic style, beige and white tones feature on walls with small cactus in terracotta pots on shelves. At the back of their store is a sewing room where you'll find the designers at work making their latest creations – a mix of formal and casual attire with a bohemian sparkle.

Via Santa Monaca 2

Mon–Sat
10.15am–7.30pm
Sun 11am–7.30pm

inexpensive

347 897 4286

W
www.shophellowonderful.com

Fine

Stefano Bemer

The finest bespoke men's shoes in the city.

In search of the perfect Italian shoe, Stefano Bemer started his business in 1983. Using artisan traditions of Florentine shoemaking, bespoke, made-to-order and ready-to-wear pairs of exquisite handcrafted footwear for men are created in tailored Oxford style lace-ups in box calf leather and suede boots or loafers with optional buckles and tassels. Bespoke orders can be made via their 'Express Lane' with fittings within two working days and delivery within ten weeks.

Stefano famously trained actor Daniel Day-Lewis as a cobbler after he fell in love with Florence and shoemaking whilst on holiday, then spent eight months as Stefano's apprentice. Now run by the same lauded leather family behind Scuola Del Cuoio (see p.109), Stefano's designs are maintained by a team of craftsmen and former pupils.

Via di San Niccolò 2

Mon–Sat
10am–7pm

€
expensive

055 046 0476

W
www.stefanobemer.com

Alessandro Dari

Enter the wonderland of this uniquely Florentine jewellery maestro.

Florence has a long history of exceptional goldsmiths and Alessandro Dari's studio is a rare space dedicated to traditional techniques of jewellery creation, with the rich atmosphere of an antique Renaissance atelier. Dari's crafted works of art, exquisite in design and execution, are not pieces you will find anywhere else in the world.

The workshop sits beneath a wooden mezzanine cluttered with shelves of tools and raw materials, while glass cabinets are filled with precious, glittering bejewelled pieces. The intricate detail of his crown rings or crosses embellished with coloured stones are inspired by the landmarks of the city. As pieces are one-of-a-kind, prices can reach into four figures, however silver creations start at €200. In 2001 the workshop was given the illustrious title of 'Museo Bottega' from the Cultural Ministry in Rome.

Via di San Niccolò 115r

055 244 747

Mon–Sat
10.30am–7.30pm
Sun 11am–7.30pm

expensive

Il Torchio

*Exquisite stationery made by hand, using traditional
Florentine techniques.*

—

Florence is famed for traditional bookbinding and paper products and a beautiful notebook is an authentic take-home purchase. Behind the gleaming glass shopfront with Il Torchio engraved on the glass is a book and paper-lover's paradise. Antique wooden cabinet shelving is lined with leather-bound books and colourful marble-effect paper made using traditions spanning hundred of years. An old press sits in the centre of the store while the main counter table has a cluster of works-in-progress by artisan Erin Ciulla, within her half-shop, half-studio.

Erin first came to Florence in 2005, immersing herself in the traditional bookbinding techniques of Florence and mastering her craft under the tutorage of Anna Anichini, the original owner of Il Torchio. Heading home to Canada a year later, Erin felt the pull of Florence so she returned to Il Torchio to fulfill her creative passion. When Anna retired, Erin took charge of the store, which has been at this location since 1980, continuing on the traditions and techniques which have been in Florence for centuries.

Via de' Bardi 17

Mon–Fri
9.30am–1.30pm,
2.30–7pm

inexpensive

W

055 23 42 862

Sat 9.30am–1.30pm

www.legatoriailtorchio.com

Fine

SUBLIME

Florence is a culture capital with art and architecture at its core. It's easy to get lost for days in its array of museums, a heady mix of classic and contemporary collections housed in some of the grandest buildings in Europe. First time visitors should cover the must-do museums yet venture beyond the well-worn routes within them – Uffizi Gallery and Galleria dell'Accademia have rooms to swoon over, away from the iconic masterpieces. Galleries like Gucci Garden and Museo Salvatore Ferragamo celebrate the city's fashion heritage and film buffs should head to Fondazione Zeffirelli. For history lovers, discover 300 years of the city's past in one action-packed hour with a theatre performance in a former nunnery – The Medici Dynasty Show. From political art in a 16th-century palace, summer sculpture at a former Renaissance fort or street art seen within the artist's secluded studio, Florence has artistic treasures at every turn.

—

Palazzo Vecchio

*The seat of power in Florence is as splendid today
as it was in the 13th century.*

—

Unmissable in the corner of the east of Piazza della Signoria, Palazzo Vecchio was begun in 1299, a medieval palace with 94-metre high tower, Torre d'Arnolfo (Arnolfo Tower), that remains a city centerpiece and the political seat of Florence today (the mayor's office has been here since 1872). Although now mainly a museum, it is the symbol of the Republic and still the seat of the City Council.

Stately room, Salone dei Cinquecento, built in 1494, was created by Girolamo Savonarola for a grand council to have 500 members, and is 52 metres in length. Legend has it that works by Michelangelo and Da Vinci were lost in its 15th-century redesign. In more in recent times, film buffs will know it from its dramatic inclusion in the Hollywood film, *Inferno*, based on the book by Dan Brown. Visit the Medici apartments where the family lived until the mid-1500s, before they moved south to Palazzo Pitti (see p.163). Climbing the Arnolfo Tower is worth the legwork for its stunning views over Florence. Also, don't miss the Lion House where Cosimo the Elder kept his collection of lions for festivities during visits from dignitaries. And lastly, make sure to take a peek at the copy of Michelangelo's statue *David* elegantly standing out front since 1910.

Piazza della Signoria

Daily
(except Thurs)

€10 (€14 with tower)

055 276 8325

9am–7pm

Until 11pm in summer

Thurs 9am–2pm

W

www.museicivici
fiorentini.comune.fi.it

Sublime

Il Grande Museo del Duomo

720 years of Florentine history under one iconic roof.

—

Cattedrale di Santa Maria del Fiore, the cathedral of Florence, is affectionately known as the Duomo. What began in 1296 and took 150 years to build, it was only complete when Filippo Brunelleschi built its terracotta dome, considered an engineering marvel, in 1436. The dome acts as beacon over the rooftops of the city with many flocking to climb to its peak, navigating the maze-like corridors that lead to its 114-metre high crescendo. Today its brilliant facade of white, green and rose marble is one to marvel at.

Il Grande Museo del Duomo is housed in the original Opera (organisation) headquarters, constructed by Brunelleschi in 1432. A recent three year and €45-million facelift created a museum to delve into the Duomo's design and construction. Over three floors 25 state-of-the-art rooms display 750 works of art, including a stunning life-size model of the cathedral's first facade re-creating the original design by architect Arnolfo di Cambio. Artwork by Ghiberti, Donatello and Michelangelo is on show, seamlessly mixing the modern infrastructure with antiquities and priceless works of art, including the original Baptistery doors, *Gates of Paradise*.

Piazza del Duomo 9

055 230 2885

Daily 9am–7pm
Closed first Tuesday of
the month

€18 (combined ticket to
Baptistery, Campanile and
museum)

W

www.museumflorence.com

Sublime

Uffizi Gallery

Find Caravaggio and the naked dwarf in the city's
finest gallery.

—

The oldest public gallery in the world, Uffizi is the art museum of Florence, housing thousands of 13th- to 18th-century artworks. Attributed to 16th-century Grand Duke Francesco I de' Medici who was responsible for the first museum arrangement, the collection now includes the likes of Giotto, Michelangelo, Botticelli, Da Vinci, Raphael, Titian and Caravaggio. It's one of the city's busiest spaces and a must-see, best in the cooler months when the large groups are out of season. In summer, book ahead to reserve an allotted time to ensure entry. Plan your visit by room rather than attempting to see all artworks in one day.

I recommend the less-travelled rooms that offer exquisite pieces away from the masses. In rooms 96–99 you'll see Caravaggio's version of wine god *Bacchus* and *Sacrifice of Isaac*, in his signature chiaroscuro style. In Room 65, find Renaissance favourite, Agnolo Bronzino's *The Dwarf Morgante*, a two-sided life-sized portrait of the famed Medici court jester resplendent in his birthday suit. The collection of ancient Greek and Roman sculpture includes the *Boar* (famously copied by sculptor Pietro Tacca in the 17th century and positioned in Mercato Nuovo). Don't miss the Tribuna, an octagonal room created for Francesco I with a dome encrusted with shells that dazzles against the blood-red coloured walls. The cafe terrace on the second floor offers panoramic views over Piazza della Signoria, a worthy stop for a coffee or cocktail after exploring the gallery's colossal artistic heritage.

📍 Piazzale degli Uffizi 6	🕐 Tues–Sun 8.15am–6.50pm	€ €20 (€12 Nov–Feb)
📞 055 294 883		W www.uffizi.it

Ponte Vecchio

Be bedazzled by the Old Bridge of Florence.

—

No trip to Florence is complete without lingering on the Ponte Vecchio. First documented in 996, the famed bridge's medieval structure dates from the 14th century and is a quintessential city landmark. Popular with travellers who gather to admire the jewellery stores, it's best enjoyed early morning as the shops open their wooden shutters or come dusk after retail hours when the bridge comes alive with buskers singing well into the night.

Linking the northern neighbourhoods to Oltrarno, it once housed a marketplace of butchers, fishmongers and tanneries, with the glittering jewel shops having been in situ since a 1593 decree by Ferdinand I. Their 17th-century back-shops precariously perch over the river Arno while above the Vasari Corridor, once a private walkway for the Medici built in 1565, links Palazzo Vecchio to Palazzo Pitti. Surviving bombing during World War Two, it's the oldest existing bridge in the city.

Ponte Vecchio

Daily
24-hours

Free

Museo Salvatore Ferragamo

A homage to the Italian shoe maestro and his legacy.

—

The fashion house of Ferragamo and Florence are synonymous, and although founder Salvatore Ferragamo was born near Naples, it was the Tuscan capital he would eventually call home. Having begun his shoe career at the tender age of 11, Salvatore opened his first shop age just 13. He moved to the USA with one of his brothers during the 1920s and it was in California, and during the Hollywood heyday, that he found fame. He opened the 'Hollywood Boot Shop' in 1923 and swiftly became 'shoemaker to the stars'.

Returning to Italy during the 1930s, it was in Florence that his life's work really took shape, renting two workshops and a shop in Palazzo Spini Feroni, a grand medieval building that remains the company's headquarters today. Even if you don't invest in a pair of shoes, visit the museum, tucked in the basement, where you can delve into the world of Salvatore and the stars. On display are his Art Deco designs, light cork wedges, stilettos, and his heels made famous by Marilyn Monroe and Audrey Hepburn. With a permanent exhibition plus regular one-off shows, this museum is a must-do for the fashion-focused.

Piazza di Santa Trinita 5r

055 356 2846

Daily
10am–7.30pm

€9

www.ferragamo.com

Sublime

Gucci Garden

*Celebrating almost 100 years of the Florentine
fashion house.*

—

Florence has an illustrious fashion heritage and the launch of Gucci Garden (formerly Gucci Museo) celebrates the famed fashion house's legacy. Housed in historic 14th-century Palazzo della Mercanzia, it's a whimsical fashion wonderland set over two floors with six themed spaces including rooms dedicated to collaborations with artists, the inaugural exhibition was a union between Icelandic singer, Björk, and Gucci creative director, Alessandro Michele.

Items dating back to the label's inception, almost 100 years, celebrate former designers, including Tom Ford's glamorous gowns, while 'GUCCIFICATION' explores the history of Gucci's iconic logo. In the retail store, exclusive Gucci Garden products are on sale, items not available in any other Gucci store. The gallery's redesign is representative of the label's current brand aesthetic: colourful and incredibly eccentric. Beyond fashion, there is food with famed three-Michelin-star Italian chef Massimo Bottura in charge of the Gucci Osteria (see p.63) nestled on the ground floor.

Piazza della Signoria 10

055 7592 7010

Mon–Fri
10am–7.30pm
Sat–Sun
10am–8pm

€8

W

www.gucci.com

Palazzo Strozzi

*Avant-garde exhibitions in a 16th-century
Florentine palazzo.*

—

From 1538 until 1937, Palazzo Strozzi remained in private ownership, home to the prominent family of the same name, and one of the finest examples of Renaissance architecture in Florence. Today it is a hot spot for contemporary exhibitions in a city traditionally focused on classical art. Its centerpiece is its grand courtyard, which you can walk through and admire without ticket admission. Here there's music events on Thursdays (during its weekly late-night opening), plus a chic bistro-cafe for caffeinated or cocktail treats.

Strozzi's shows are always innovative. A recent exhibition was The Florence Experiment, a collaboration between artist Carsten Höller and scientist Stefano Mancuso. They installed two 20-metre slides for visitors to cascade down the courtyard facade within the palazzo. Other shows have ranged from Chinese activist artist, Ai Weiwei, to works by Van Gogh. La Strozzina, its mini basement gallery, often hosts exhibition offshoot shows while Bottege Strozzi, the bookstore run by Marsilio Editori, is filled with a colourful collection of contemporary publications. Scheduled guided tours are also available.

Piazza degli Strozzi

055 264 5155

Fri–Wed
10am–8pm
Thurs
10am–11pm

€

€12

W

www.palazzostrozzi.org

Casamonti Collection

An extraordinary personal collection.

Roberto Casamonti, a Florentine art collector and owner of Tornabuoni Arte, which launched in 1981, opened this exhibition in 2018 within the usually private Palazzo Bartolini Salimbeni. Having built an impressive art empire of over 5000 works during almost four decades, Casamonti's collection is a welcome addition to the city's impressive art scene. It currently shows 250 acquisitions featuring 20th-century art from the early 1900s to the 1960s, displayed across five rooms. From Futurism and Cubism to Bauhaus, works include Picasso, Kandinsky, Klee, Boccioni and Warhol.

It's also a way to see inside Palazzo Bartolini Salimbeni, the first palace in Florence built according to the 'Roman' Renaissance style and designed by architect Baccio d'Agnolo in the 1520s.

Piazza di Santa Trinita 1

055 602 030

Wed–Sun
11.30am–7pm

€10

www.collezione
robertocasamonti.com

The Medici Dynasty Show

Sex, drugs and the Renaissance in one action-packed hour.

On 24 June 1737, Gian Gastone, the last Medici Grand Duke, was on his deathbed in Palazzo Pitti. With his estranged sister, Anna Maria Luisa, they concocted the Family Pact, ensuring all works of art are kept in Florence, never to be sold off. From the 14th to 18th centuries, the Medicis were politically powerful, astute in business and wealthy with many rivals. They commissioned some of the most magnificent buildings and greatest works of art in Florence. Their Family Pact arguably made Florence the great Renaissance art city it is today.

In this two-performer play, 300 years of Medici influence is detailed in an action-packed 60-minute dialogue. A true story at its theatrical finest, it's an entertaining way to understand the city's history and the legacy of one family's lasting dynasty.

Via Faenza 48

Show time 7pm

€30

349 131 0441

W

www.medicidynasty.com

Galleria dell'Accademia

Fawn at the feet of the original statue of David.

—

When it comes to Florence, it's fair to say two of the city's most famous sons are Michelangelo and *David*. In fact, *David* is the single most mentioned artwork in all English language literature, with many copies throughout the world. Seeing the five-metre marble statue of Michelangelo's creation is, for some, life changing with grown adults reduced to tears. So a visit to the Galleria dell'Accademia is a must-do to see the original. It's a dramatic walk down the Hall of the Prisoners, past Michelangelo's unfinished statues first commissioned for Pope Julius II in 1505, before you find yourself fawning at *David's* feet. He's tucked at the end of the Tribune perched on a pedestal surrounded by other 16th-century artworks of his generation.

The Accademia holds many other artworks of significance and is renowned for its Mannerist works and Florentine Gothic paintings of the 13th and 14th centuries. Make time to see inside Gipsoteca Bartolini, a room filled with plaster cast models by Lorenzo Bartolini, its layout fashioned on the workshop of Galleria Romanelli (see p.166). In a side room, the Museum of Musical Instruments accommodates 50 antique harpsichords, string and wind instruments, a viola from 1690 and a pianoforte, the original piano design by Bartolomeo Cristofori for the Medicis.

📍	🕐	€
Via Ricasoli 58–60	Tues–Sun 8.15am–6.50pm	€8
📞		W
055 238 8609		www.galleria accademiafirenze.beniculturali.it

Sublime

Fondazione Zeffirelli

The city's most famous filmmaker is celebrated in
true theatrical style.

—

Internationally acclaimed director Franco Zeffirelli has had an illustrious career spanning seven decades. He is known for films such as *Tea with Mussolini, Hamlet, Jane Eyre* and *The Taming of the Shrew* and for working with Hollywood icons like Elizabeth Taylor and Richard Burton. His 1968 version of *Romeo and Juliet* won him an Oscar nomination. Having produced 18 films, staged 31 theatre performances and brought to life more than 100 operatic works, this celebrated writer, scenographer, costume designer and director now has a dedicated museum in the heart of his hometown.

Within Complex of Saint Firenze, a former monastery of the Filippini Fathers, the exhibition starts from Zeffirelli's humble roots in 1953 and is divided into 20 'chapters' by room. Almost 300 sketches are displayed, along with posters, fliers, costumes, set-design models, original drawings, and behind-the-scenes photographs taken on-set. The ground floor hosts a quaint tearoom that extends into the palazzo courtyard, while its neighbouring bookstore sells Zeffirelli books and film paraphernalia.

Piazza di San Firenze 5

055 281 038

Fri–Wed
10am–6pm

€10

W
www.fondazionefrancozeffirelli.com

Palazzo Pitti

Discover three dynasties tracing 500 years
of grand regal glory.

—

Originally built by banker Luca Pitti in the 15th century, Palazzo Pitti was purchased in 1550 by Eleanor of Toledo, wife of Grand Duke Cosimo I de' Medici, who desired a more modern home away from the 'old' apartments of Palazzo Vecchio (see p.143). They doubled the building in size to become the most grandiose palace in Florence, a symbol of their power and the new Grand Ducal residence. The facade is striking and imposing when approached from the palace entrance, its stone piazza a popular spot to sun yourself between gallery visits.

Within Pitti are five museums, making it the largest exhibition complex in Florence. Treasury of the Grand Dukes has exquisite quadrature frescoes and priceless jewellery including 16th-century gems once belonging to Anna Maria Luisa de' Medici. Upstairs is Gallery of Modern Art, Museum of Costume and Fashion (see p.165), and the Royal and Imperial Apartments, kept in their original 18th-century style since the House of Lorraine–Habsburg called Pitti home. In the Palatine Gallery 500 masterpieces by Raphael, Titian, Caravaggio and Rubens, once part of the Medici collection, hang in ostentatiously decorated rooms. Napoleon, in his quest to expand the French Empire, used the palace as his Florence base between 1799 and 1814 (his private bathroom remains) while out back, the Boboli Gardens (see p.184) is a green respite from the city's cobbled streets.

⚲	⊙	€
Piazza de Pitti 1	Tues–Sun	€16 (€10 Nov-Feb)
	8.15am–6.50pm	
☏		W
055 294 883		www.uffizi.it

Sublime

Museum of Costume and Fashion

Florentine fashion from the 1500s to present day.

—

If you have a passion for fashion or are looking for a unique gallery experience, Museum of Costume and Fashion (Museo della Moda e del Costume, formerly the Costume Gallery) is a captivating experience with glamorous gowns and accessories, from the 1500s to present day. Founded in 1983, as the first State-run museum in Italy dedicated to the history of fashion, you'll find a treasure trove of pieces housed in the southern wing, Palazzina della Meridiana, of Palazzo Pitti (see p.163).

The earliest pieces on display are the funeral clothing of Cosimo I de' Medici, Eleonora of Toledo and their son Garzia de' Medici that have been completely restored from their decayed 16th-century condition. Other garments include vintage Chanel, Gucci, Versace, and Prada, custom-made Florentine and Neapolitan bridal gowns and costume jewellery and accessories dating from the 18th century. Many of the pieces are borrowed from the private collections of Italian personalities in fashion and art. The mannequins used to display each outfit have been custom-made to fit the garment's original owner. Also featured are design sketches and drawings to tell the design tale of the garments on display.

Piazza de Pitti 1

Tues–Sun
8.15am–6.50pm

€16 (€10 Nov–Feb)

055 294 883

W

www.uffizi.it/en/pitti-palace/costume-and-fashion-museum

Sublime

Galleria Romanelli

Explore Florence of the past in one of the oldest working sculpture studios in Europe.

In the Romanelli family since 1860, today their Galleria is run by Raffaello, who specialises in portrait busts. The studio uses traditional techniques to create bronzes cast in the Lost Wax Method designs. They create reproductions of classic works from the family's extensive archive and host courses on clay modelling, plaster casting and marble carving.

Originally a 15th-century church, the gallery houses 8-metre high 19th-century sculptures under 16-metre high arched ceilings. Hundreds of sculptures made by generations over two centuries attract art lovers, collectors, architects, and interior designers. Once the studio of famed 19th-century sculptor Lorenzo Bartolini, you'll find the gallery at Romanelli replicated within Galleria dell'Accademia (see p.159).

Borgo San Frediano 70

055 239 6047

Mon–Fri
10am–1pm,
2–6pm

Free

W
www.raffaello
romanelli.com

Clet Abraham Studio

A little French fancy, via art, in Florence.

A Francophile firmly planted in Florence for two decades, Clet Abraham is synonymous with street art, launching take-overs of street signs, much to the local council's dismay. His guerilla-style operation has sparked a following of his artistic talents.

Clet uses removable stickers to reinterpret street signs, so look up when walking through Florence to find them, adding a little whimsy, charm and provocativeness to what, Clet felt, was a uniformed approach to living. A 'No Through Road' signage is reimagined to become a crucifix with a hanging Jesus; a 'This Way' arrow turned into Pinocchio's nose. In his pocket-sized studio, you can see and buy his designs, from original artwork to stickers, postcards and T-shirts.

Via dell'Olmo 8

331 232 7335

Daily
10.30am–1.30pm,
3–7.30pm

€

Free

W

www.facebook.com/
clet.abraham

Forte di Belvedere

*Contemporary sculpture in the grounds of a classic
fortress with striking views to match.*

—

Built in the 1590s by the ruling Medici family, Forte di Belvedere was a
defensive stronghold, in part a Renaissance military base, perched high on
the southernmost hill in Florence. After being closed to the public for years,
the Forte re-opened in 2013 and has become a go-to during the summer
months to enjoy the latest sculpture exhibition that weaves through its
garden and grounds. Its name translates to 'fort of the beautiful view' and for
good reason – an outdoor art space to be seen, experienced and enjoyed.

With a focus on contemporary art and pioneers of sculpture, past exhibitions
have included British-born Antony Gormley, Belgian Jan Fabre and avant-
garde Italian artist, Eliseo Mattiacci. Although the outside spaces are the
main event, more pieces are housed within the cream-coloured villa that
sits on the centre of the hill. A pop-up bar is perfectly positioned for sunset
cocktails offering some of the most spectacular views of Florence and over
neighbouring Boboli Gardens (see p.184).

Via di San Leonardo 1

055 276 8224

Tues–Sun
11am–8pm
(last entry 7pm)
Summer months only

€3

W

www.museicivici
fiorentini.comune.fi.it

Sublime

NINE

*Florence is a city that delights the senses – from the
tantalising tastes of trattorias, wood-fired oven pizza joints
and mouthwatering gelato, to the fresh smells of its green
spaces, the idyllic spots where you can breathe in scented air
away from the city's cobblestone streets. Beyond the artisan
stores and iconic Florentine brands, you'll find treasures
at my favourite bustling markets, while Florence's ancient
lanes are buzzing with beauty salons so that you can enjoy
a little pampering amid all that food and shopping. If you're
a nightowl, dive into Florence's nightlife – from jazz clubs to
storytelling evenings, or simply enjoy a sunset with a Spritz in
hand. For shut-eye, seek a dreamy boutique sleepover under a
fresco in a former palace. NINE features nine lists of the best
Florence has to offer.*

—

MARKETS

Perusing markets around Florence is a wondrous way to while away time in true Italian fashion. From food, to antique furnishings, leather goods and flowers, there is a day and venue to suit all tastes.

Mercato di Sant'Ambrogio
Foodie heaven for those seeking an authentic experience, this morning market is mainly filled with green grocers selling their fresh produce. Within the iron-clad building by architect Giuseppe Mengoni you'll find butchers, fishmongers and bakers all going about their daily routine. Also inside, Da Rocco serves up lunchtime plates of soups, pastas and meat dishes starting at only €4 a plate. Mon–Sat 7am–2pm.
Piazza Ghiberti
www.mercatosantambrogio.it

San Lorenzo
Outside Il Mercato Centrale (see p.67), you'll find the pedestrian streets lined with stalls selling leather and take-home trinkets, the main thoroughfare running down Via dell' Ariento starting at Piazza di San Lorenzo. This market has become rather touristy over the past decade however dive in as you may discover a little souvenir diamond amongst the generic rough.
Daily 9am–7pm.
Piazza del Mercato Centrale

Fortezza da Basso
This bustling antique market takes place on the third weekend of every month in the outer grounds of the 16th-century fort designed by Antonio da Sangallo the Younger for Alessandro de' Medici. Today you'll find an assortment of bric-a-brac, vintage furniture, oil paintings and collectables, a treasure trove of antiquities. It's always busy with local Florentines perusing the day away around the serene pond and greenery of the fort garden.
Third weekend of every month 9am–7.30pm.
Viale Strozzi
www.en.comune.fi.it

San Lorenzo

San Lorenzo

Santo Spirito

The leafy, and often lively, piazza in Santo Spirito hosts an arts and crafts market every second Sunday of the month. From handmade pottery to silverware and food items, the stalls are set up around the square's central fountain. On the third Sunday of the month, the piazza hosts its food market under the church facade; it's a leisurely way to spend a morning before a long, lazy Sunday lunch. Second and third Sunday of the month 9am–7pm.
Piazza Santo Spirito
www.en.comune.fi.it

Mercato Nuovo

Housed under the magnificent Loggia del Mercato Nuovo built for Cosimo I de' Medici in 1547, this leather market is also filled with T-shirts and souvenir trinkets. Often referred to as Mercato del Porcellino after the popular bronze wild boar statue designed by Pietro Tacca, which graces its southern wall. Legend has it if you rub its nose and offer a coin, the porcellino will bring you good luck. Daily 9am–6.30pm.
Piazza del Mercato Nuovo
www.mercatodelporcellino.it

Mercatino delle Pulci

Originally housed in Piazza dei Ciompi, this Sant'Ambrogio-based antiques market is now set up in a modern square besides the neighbourhood's food market. Stalls sell antiques, jewellery, vintage clothing, books and other collectables – you never know your luck in what you'll uncover. On the last Sunday of the month, the market spills into the adjoining streets, a festive way to end the weekend. Mon–Sat 8am–7.30pm.
Largo Pietro Annigoni
www.en.comune.fi.it

San Lorenzo

Cascine Park

As local a market as you'll find, this Tuesday morning set-up sees a stream of stalls pop up in the city's largest park. There are hundreds of sellers offering affordable clothing, shoes, household items and food, both fresh and take-away, in a no-frills environment flowing for three kilometers parallel to the river Arno. Every Tuesday 7am–2pm.

Viale Abramo Lincoln
www.en.comune.fi.it

Il Mercatale

Charming wooden stalls take over Piazza della Repubblica each month for a food feast of local farmers' produce and artisans selling quality Tuscan products. From peppery Extra Virgin olive oil to Chianti, fruity jams, cured salamis, and truffle-infused honey, the market transforms the piazza into a village-like atmosphere where you can sample food and meet the makers. First Saturday of each month 8am–8pm.

Piazza della Repubblica
www.en.comune.fi.it

Flower Market

Every Thursday morning under the portico arches, the west side of Piazza della Repubblica comes alive with seasonal blooms of flowers, ferns and other greenery. From bunches ideal for vases to potted plants, it's a worthy morning stroll just for the smells if not to take home your own bright mazzo (bouquet). Thursday 8am–2pm.

Via Pellicceria

Nine

BEAUTY

Feeling like you need a little pampering in between cultural excursions? Beauty in Florence is not limited to its art galleries.

Maniboo

Arguably the best mani/pedi in town, when Maniboo opened its purple doors its California-style treatments took the city by storm. Within its purple drawing room, four velvet banquettes are ready for manicures while out back, your tootsies are immersed in a warm bath before the polishing begins. Book ahead so you won't be disappointed.

Borgo Ognissanti 4r
www.maniboo.it

Wave

Matteo is the main man at this stylish parrucchieri (hairdressers) when it comes to my tresses, however all staff will pamper you. Within the front loggia of a grand Santo Spirito palazzo, Aveda products are used and there are other treatments like manicures and waxing upstairs. A one-stop beauty shop south of the river Arno.

Via di Santo Spirito 27
www.parrucchieriwavefirenze.com

Ziziai

This sleek salon down a backstreet near the Duomo is run by the effervescent Simone and Valeria. With over 25 years hairdressing experience, Simone is in charge of tresses while Valeria focuses on make-up. Book an appointment for this one-seat only salon.

Via dei Biffi 5r
www.ziziai.com

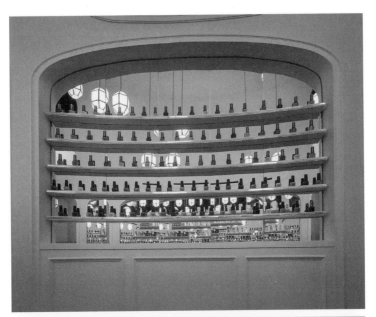

Maniboo

Ortigia

Established in 2006 by Sue Townsend, one of the founding owners of Crabtree & Evelyn, this Italian store is intoxicating. Behind the palm tree-adorned glass front door are rows of brightly coloured products inspired by Sicily and made in Tuscany. Nutty almond, lavender, Sicilian lime, orange blossom and sweet pomegranate are a few of the ranges to choose from and much of it is handmade.
Borgo San Jacopo 12r
www.ortigiasicilia.com

Silathai

Thai massage is the best jet-lag cure I know. So I run to the tranquil Silathai the minute I land in Florence to enjoy some relaxation under the arch of a fresco ceiling. Deep tissue and oil are available (€30 for 30 minutes, €60 for 60 minutes) and oils can be purchased to take home. Enjoy pandan and lemongrass tea afterwards.
Via dei Serragli 63r
www.silathaimassage.com

Aqua Flor

This perfume showroom harks back to a bygone era of Florence. Set in a 16th-century palazzo beneath glorious arched ceilings, large wooden cabinets contain rows of glass bottles filled with sensual scents. With bespoke bottles available and workshops too, experience the ambience of a salon dedicated to the fine art of perfume making. Also see p.111.
Borgo Santa Croce 6
www.florenceparfum.com

Lorenzo Villoresi

Lorenzo Villoresi

Perfume master Villoresi has been working his magic since 1990 in a secluded bottega (workshop) surrounded by scents and exotic smells from all around the world. Famed for his one-of-a-kind bottles made to order, you can visit his sleek perfume emporium hidden in a 16th-century palazzo in the quaint district of San Niccolò. With a perfume museum and academy due to open in 2019, there are many reasons to visit.
Via de' Bardi 12
www.lorenzovilloresi.it

Officina Profumo-Farmaceutica di Santa Maria Novella

Originally a monastery where monks created tinctures for health, this elegant atelier dedicated to apothecary has over 400 years of history. Under the grandeur of the Great Sales Hall, it was originally a chapel dedicated to San Niccolò di Bari, and frescoes painted by Paolino Sarti represent the fame of the Pharmacy and its products across the world. Try before you buy, from hand cream to perfumes including its namesake originally commissioned by Caterina de' Medici. Make sure to visit its ancient Antica Spezieria, the old shop dating from 1612.
Via della Scala 16
www.smnovella.com

Poesia21

With an aim to bring the Italian countryside to your body and home, these organic beauty products are 100% made in Tuscany using fresh spring herbs, rose hip berry, helichrysum, Iris Florentina and wild flowers. The range includes perfumes, bath gels, crèmes based in vegetable oils (rice, sweet almonds and sunflowers), exfoliating gels, and body oils. Scented candles are made with 100% natural ECOSOYA® wax.
Via della Spada 36r
www.poesia21.com

Nine

GELATO

Legend has it gelato was first created in Florence by Bernardo Buontalenti and with many geletarie serving fresh, innovative and mouth-watering flavours, what better place to try Italy's famous delicacy than in its birthplace?

My Sugar

When My Sugar opened in summer 2015 it was to much local applaud. Run by husband-and-wife team Alberto and Julia Bati, who pride themselves on 'made fresh daily' soft, sweet gelato, this small shop offers seasonal scoops from only €2 a cup. Try a classic like dark chocolate or in summer opt for a fruity flavour of watermelon or zesty passionfruit.

Via de Ginori 49r
https://my-sugar.business.site

Gelateria La Carraia

Opened in 1990 by twin brothers Massimo and Roberto, La Carraia fast became a favourite – and still is – with both locals and travellers alike. Artisanal ice-cream is made daily onsite in their San Frediano store with cheesecake my personal favourite. With a second shop, over the Arno River in Santa Croce on Via dei Benci (24r), now you have no excuse to not try a cone on either side of the city.

Piazza Nazario Sauro 25
www.lacarraiagroup.eu

Gelateria Della Passera

Hidden in the corner of quaint Piazza della Passera in Santo Spirito, this tiny gelateria hand-makes its daily creations from its miniscule kitchen out back. Offering a range of both milk-based and sorbet flavours, it's perfect for people who are lactose intolerant. In summer, favourites include zesty Mojito infused with lime and mint, or in the winter try nutty pistachio or velvety smooth crema.

Via Toscanella 15
www.gelaterialapassera.wordpress.com

My Sugar

Ponte Santa Trinita

It's written in the signs

Gelateria Dei Neri

On the other side of town, Gelateria dei Neri is neatly positioned among panini stores and cafes at the end of a medieval street in Santa Croce. From a glistening counter it serves an array of classic flavours like chocolate and noci (nuts) or more innovative fruity mandarin and mint, plus delicious desserts, including tempting tiramisu.

Via Dei Neri 9–11r

www.facebook.com/gelateriadeneri

Gelateria Edoardo

It's the sweet smell of its homemade cones that first hits your senses to draw you into this small gelateria opposite the Duomo (see p.145). Organic gelato is served in freshly baked waffle cones topped with scoops including signature flavour, Il Gianduia Secondo Edoardo (hazelnuts and chocolate), or in summer try the sweet peach that uses the whole fruit, including its skin, for maximum flavour.

Piazza del Duomo 45r

www.edoardobio.it

Gelateria Vivaldi

This gelateria/cafe in San Niccolò makes their sweet treats onsite – you can watch the gelati being made by hand in their mezzanine kitchen before being served in cups and cones. For zesty tastebuds, sample Arancia Rosso (blood red orange) or perhaps creamy cappuccino is more to your taste. Vivaldi also serve hot chocolate in winter, which you can sip reclined on one of their comfy sofas in their lounge out the back.

Via de' Renai 15r

www.facebook.com/GelateriaVivaldi

Gelateria Santa Trinita

In Santo Spirito, Gelateria Santa Trinita is a popular gelato destination all year round located opposite its namesake bridge south of the river Arno. Take a cup or cone filled with rich chocolate fondant or sesamo nero (black sesame seed) and sit on the bridge of Ponte Santa Trinita to take in the sweeping views of Florence. The store also has a small adjoining shop with Tuscan chocolates, wine and jams.

Piazza Frescobaldi 11–12r
www.gelateriasantatrinita.it

La Sorbetteria

Hidden away in the very local neighborhood of San Frediano, La Sorbetteria was opened in 2007 by husband-and-wife team Antonio and Elisa. Antonio's family has been making gelato and handing recipes down through the generations since 1934, and they pride themselves on producing the best flavours using only quality, local ingredients.

Piazza Torquato Tasso 11r
www.lasorbettiera.com

Antica Gelateria Fiorentina

This hole-in-the-wall gelateria in San Lorenzo has mouth-watering flavours from crunchy stracciatella (chocolate chip) to fruity flavours like fragola (strawberry), or matcha (green tea) from only €1,50 a scoop. It's a great stop after visiting the famed food and leather markets just a block away (see p.172).

Via Faenza 2a
www.gelateriafiorentina.com

GREEN SPACES

In a city made of stone, finding a green respite after a day of exploring, particularly in summer, is a rare and desired reprieve. Here's a number of hidden gems.

Boboli Gardens
This green oasis was first created as a private garden for the Medici family when they resided in Palazzo Pitti (see p.163) from the mid-16th century. There are 11 acres of parkland, much of it manicured, with fountains, modern and classical sculpture, and maze-like shrubbery. With a rather hefty stand-alone ticket price, the garden is worth popping into after visiting Palazzo Pitti as it's included in the ticket price.
Piazza Pitti 1
www.uffizi.it/en/boboli-garden

Rose Garden
With over 400 rose species in this secluded San Niccolò garden, it's the ideal green space especially come spring. Open from sunrise until sunset, between the blooms are modern sculptures by Belgian artist Jean-Michel Folon, while to the east a simple yet tranquil Japanese garden has sweeping views towards the Duomo. For the active, a light hike to the highest tip offers a quiet location perfect for an afternoon picnic.
Viale Giuseppe Poggi 2

Bardini Gardens
Most travellers flock to neighbouring, popular Boboli Gardens (see above), however, five minutes' east is the garden of Villa Bardini in all its manicured glory – a quintessential Italian Renaissance garden with a sweeping baroque staircase weaving its way south towards the Arno and Via di San Niccolò. Come during spring to see its amazing wisteria pergola in full bloom. Its simple yet elegant loggia, at its highest peak, offers stunning views over Florence. And as it also houses a small bar, order a glass of Rosé to make the view that little sweeter.
Costa San Giorgio 2

Rose Garden

Horticultural Garden

Iris Garden

Open for only month every year, the Iris Garden is a must-do for the flower aficionado if in Florence in late April (check their website for annual opening dates). The Iris Fiorentina flower is the official Florence symbol. The garden is just to the east of popular lookout Piazzale Michelangelo overlooking the city, its views are particularly dazzling come sunset.

Viale Michelangiolo

www.societaitalianairis.com

Horticultural Garden

To the north of the city centre, just outside the old city walls, with its elegant 19th-century Victorian greenhouse, Horticultural Garden is popular in the summer months where the local hipster crowd flock to a pop-up bar on hot balmy nights. Take a stroll to its most northern point for spectacular views of the city and Duomo. Or swing by for the free music in summer from 7pm.

Via Vittorio Emanuele II 4

www.societatoscanaorticultura.it

Cascine Park

The largest public space in Florence at 395 acres, Cascine was once a hunting ground for the Medici during their 300-year reign. Today it hosts weekly markets (see p.175) and summer music concerts, while runners love the exercise lanes to enjoy the sunrise along the banks of the river Arno. Come summer, locals flock to the park's public swimming pool, Le Pavoniere.

Piazzale delle Cascine

http://parcodellecascine.comune.fi.it

Torrigiani Garden

Torrigiani Garden

The largest private garden in a walled European city, with almost 17 acres of hidden greenery, Torrigiani Gardens' central feature is the neo-gothic tower at 22-metres high, built to study the stars in 1824. The garden is open by appointment with guided tours offered by family members, so book in advance. On occasion they host special events. Should you be looking for a sleepover, AdAstra (see p.204) boasts a terrace overlooking the grounds and two of its rooms are neatly nestled amongst its foliage.

Via dei Serragli 144
www.giardinotorrigiani.it

Piazza Tasso

At this neighbourhood piazza in Oltrarno, you'll normally find local school kids playing basketball in the courtyards by late afternoon. It's a small yet green respite away from the maddening crowds in high season. With La Sorbetteria (see p.183) gelateria opposite and a local's bar, Aurora, tucked into a medieval wall tower, these are two good reasons to venture this far south.

Piazza Torquato Tasso
www.firenze-oltrarno.net

San Miniato al Monte

Not technically a green space, however this church and working monastery is well worth visiting to see Florence's vista at its finest, and is a tranquil place for contemplation. You'll see the perfect blend of city meets countryside as olive groves and cypress trees engulf the southern part of Florence. The church celebrated its 1000-year birthday in 2018 and continues to host daily mass, often with spine-tingling Gregorian chants. Out back, the cemetery is a serene affair with elegant tombstones and less-travelled gravel paths surrounded by rambling Tuscan vegetation.

Via delle Porte Sante 34
www.sanminiatoalmonte.it

Nine

APERITIVO

Aperitivo is an institution in Florence, a time to meet friends and catch up over a drink or two come dusk. Essentially cocktail hour, many venues also offer small plates of food (some free!), an Italian custom to enjoy a light bite with your delectable drink of choice.

SE.STO
Your visit to Florence won't be complete without watching the Tuscan sunset, and where better than on the rooftop of five-star hotel, Westin Excelsior with cocktail in hand. With 180-degree panoramic views down the river Arno, it's been wow-ing visitors with its jaw-dropping sunsets over the terracotta roofs of the city for years. At aperitivo hour your stiff drink will come with a free buffet of fine food, enough for a meal, offered every evening from 7pm.
Piazza Ognissanti 3
www.sestoonarno.com

Tamerò
After a day exploring Palazzo Pitti (see p.163) or Boboli Gardens (see p.184), discover nearby Tamerò. With graffiti-covered walls, DJs and live music, Tamerò is more than just a pasta bar. From within a converted former mechanics workshop, the bar serves classic drinks like Spritz with an accompanying buffet from 6.30pm of pasta, cous cous and salads. Tables spill onto Piazza Santo Spirito, the best seats in the summer months. Also see p.85.
Piazza Santo Spirito 11r
www.tamero.it

Odeon Bistro
The Odeon is a classic 1930s' theatre-style cinema that shows English-language films most days. Its bistro-bar is an elegant boudoir space with velvet chairs, banquettes and dim lighting by Palazzo Strozzi (see p.155). For the price of your glass of wine or a cocktail, tuck into a buffet spread of fine meats, cheeses, panini and hot food from 7pm before taking in the lastest film in the theatre next door.
Piazza degli Strozzi 8r
www.odeonbistro.it

Sei Divino

amblè

Tamerò

Le Volpi e L'Uva   *Sei Divino*

Sabor Cubano

A little slice of Havana in Florence, Sabor Cubano is a miniscule bar hidden in the arches opposite Florence's Il Mercato Centrale (see p.67), offering a spicy drinks' menu specialising in rum-based cocktails. Head barman Lopez makes classic margaritas complete with black Himalayan salt rim, or try a zesty mojito infused with his freshly made juices like grapefruit or pomegranate.

Via Sant'Antonino 64r
www.saborcubanofirenze.com

Move On

This hip bar and record store is smack bang in the centre of Florence opposite the Duomo. The ground floor features a wood-panelled bar serving craft beers and a classic Italian food selection, while upstairs you can sift through rows of new records, reissues, second-hand vinyl, rare items, music books and accessories.

Piazza San Giovanni 1r
www.moveonfirenze.com

amblé

Escape the hustle of Ponte Vecchio to this vintage shop-cum-bar in a quiet courtyard just a block north from the river Arno. It serves cocktails but that's not all – everything in the store is for sale. Ask your barman for his cocktail suggestions which change depending on the season. Or simply opt for a classic Spritz served in a jam jar along with amblé's home-baked bread fries. Also see p.28.

Chiasso dei del Bene
www.amble.it

amblè

Sei Divino

With an extensive range of quality Italian wines, Neri Vignozzi pours glasses from 200 labels with 100 to taste by the glass, in this cosy wine bar a block from the river Arno. The food menu changes daily, serving Aperigourmet: with quality cheeses, cold cuts and hot dishes freshly prepared by their in-house chef. Also see p.33.
Borgo Ognissanti 42r
www.seidivinofirenze.it

Fusion Bar in Gallery Hotel Art

Pop by this hotel tucked in a quaint courtyard by Ponte Vecchio to peruse the latest exhibition, open to all, with David Lachapelle, Steven Klein and Andy Warhol featuring in the past. The hotel's Fusion Bar is ideal for a pre-dinner cocktail – try their Herbal Martini based in gin with 47 botanicals from India and drops of green Chartreuse, a liquor obtained from 130 different herbs and prepared by local monks. Also see p.206.
Vicolo dell'Oro 5
www.lungarnocollection.com

Le Volpi e L'Uva

A favourite with foodies and locals alike, it specialises in small wine producers from Italy. Famed for its succulent crostone bread slices plus boards of cheeses, cured meats and breads from small specialty local producers. Take a pew at the inside bar or at the few streetside tables to sample glasses of wine from local vineyards. Also see p.51.
Piazza dei Rossi 1r
www.levolpieluva.com

PIZZA

Wood-fired oven pizza, 72-hour slow-rise dough, Neapolitan and Tuscan toppings, eat yours like a local on church steps or in a converted car mechanics former workshop.

Braciere Malatesta

The Baglioni family has been firing up their wood-fire oven in San Lorenzo since 1954 and dedicated to pizza perfection ever since. The menu features typical Italian toppings like Margherita (tomato, mozzarella, basil) or Four Seasons (tomato, mozzarella, olives, ham, mushrooms). Try one of the specials – the Count Mascetti, topped with tomatoes, truffle burrata cheese and Tuscan lard. Also see p.68.
Via Nazionale 36
www.bracieremalatesta.com

Gusta

The Gusta brothers have brought their southern style pizza-making to Florence with a classic Italian-style joint popular with students and travellers, you'll often see queues by the dining room door before opening hours. It's shared seating inside or make like the locals and take your pizza to the steps of the neighbouring church of Santo Spirito.
Via Maggio 46r
www.facebook.com/GustapizzaFirenze

SimBIOsi

Biological wholegrain stone ground flour is used for the pizza bases in this San Lorenzo diner – they don't call the restaurant SimBIOsi for no reason. Priding themselves on quality produce, toppings are inventive with Salsiccia e broccoli (handmade sausage, broccoli, mozzarella) or pea hummus, prawns, walnuts and stracciatella cheese. There's a good list of artisan beers and organic wine is also available.
Via dei Ginori 56r
www.simbiosi.bio

Braciere Malatesta

Tamerò Pizzeria

Tamerò Pizzeria

The team behind pasta restaurant Tamerò (see p.85) have transformed the
back of their re-vamped car mechanic workshop in Santo Spirito into a
pizzeria serving freshly baked pizza from a wood-fired oven. Classic toppings
fill the menu with popular veggie options including eggplant and mozzarella.
Or try the salty explosion of the Napoli – tomato, mozzarella, anchovies,
capers and oregano.
Borgo Tegolaio 22r
https://la-pizzeria-del-tamero.business.site

Santarpia

Named after the original pizzaiolo (pizza-maker) Giovanni Santarpia, (who
was awarded the Tre spicchi, the highest recognition by food guide, Gambero
Rosso, in 2018), Santarpia prides itself on its dough bases that have gently
risen for 48 hours before being kneaded into your pizza. Want to be local?
Try the Florentine lampredotto (tripe) topping or the more classic Margherita
that uses tomatoes from Vesuvius and buffalo mozzarella from Campania.
Largo Pietro Annigoni 9c
www.santarpia.biz

SUD

Fresh fast food is what the upstairs food hall in Il Mercato Centrale (see p.67)
is all about, and SUD whips up piping hot made-to-order Neapolitan-style
pizza from its wood-fired oven with only five select topping choices, the
Margherita reigning pizza supreme.
Piazza del Mercato Centrale
www.mercatocentrale.it

Berberè

Berberè

Brothers Matteo and Salvatore hail from Calabria and opened their first pizzeria in 2010 (which was awarded Tre spicchi by food guide Gambero Rosso in 2018). This San Frediano outpost, also has a focus on artisanal pizza made with sourdough that is rested for at least 24 hours. Toppings are seasonal and many organic with each pizza sliced into eight pieces to encourage sharing between friends. They also have gluten-free options.
Piazza de' Nerli 1
www.berberepizza.it

L'antica pizzeria da Michele

Their original Naples pizzeria is lauded by locals, and praised in the book, *Eat Pray Love* by Elizabeth Gilbert. Da Michele has been a forefather of pizza making since 1870. This recently opened outpost in Florence, opposite the central market in San Lorenzo, makes only six pizza styles from its wood-fired oven. Tuck into a Neapolitan – tomato, mozzarella, anchovies, oregano and capers – as a nod to the venue's origins.
Piazza del Mercato Centrale 22r
www.pizzeriadamichelefirenze.it

l'Pizzacchiere

Dough is given 72 hours to rise, a show of how seriously the pizzaiolo (pizza makers) are about creating their Neapolitan-style pizzas. With 45 pizzas to choose from the menu is vast – from calzone to a gourmet list including Honeymoon – buffalo mozzarella, black truffle, pecorino cheese, drizzled with delicate orange blossom honey. As service is swift, it's a good express lunch en route to Forte di Belvedere (see p.169) or the Rose Garden (see p.184).
Via San Miniato 2
www.pizzacchiere.com

Nine

TRATTORIA

From hole-in-the-wall cosy eateries to Mamma and Papa traditional Tuscan, dining in trattorias means that you get local, classic, comfort cuisine.

Sergio Gozzi

It's easy to miss this historic restaurant, serving since 1915, wedged between the leather shops in bustling San Lorenzo. This is atraditional trattoria serving hearty Tuscan dishes of warming ribollita (bread soup), peposo (stewed beef) and coniglio (rabbit) making it an ideal lunch spot.

Piazza San Lorenzo 8r

Trattoria dell'Orto

This family-run restaurant in San Frediano serves up plates of delicious pasta and Florentine favourites – try the tagliatelle with speck and artichoke, and roasted meats such as the sublime pollo al mattone (brick-roasted chicken), all washed down with local house wine. Service can be slow yet that's part of the charm – don't rush but just savour the food and dining experience, be it for lunch or dinner.

Via dell'Orto 35a
www.trattoriadellorto.com

Ristorante del Fagioli

Relax over a hearty dinner at Fagioli, a family run restaurant in Santa Croce renowned for its classic Tuscan plates including Bistecca alla Fiorentina, a thick T-bone steak lightly seared on both sides that only comes one way – bloody. Pair it with white beans cooked in rosemary and crisp potatoes for the perfect Italian feast.

Corso dei Tintori 47r

Sergio Gozzi

Sergio Gozzi

Ristorante del Fagioli

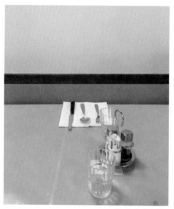

Trattoria Sabatino

Trattoria Sabatino

Nestled beside the medieval gate in San Frediano, Sabatino has been a trusted local eatery since 1956, serving up quality traditional dishes at very reasonable prices. You're more likely to sit next to a Florentine than a tourist to enjoy spaghetti al sugo, roast veal and tiramisu a steal for €3,50.

Via Pisana 2r

www.trattoriasabatino.it

Osteria Vini e Vecchi Sapori

Near Uffizi Gallery (see p.147) and Bargello (see p.19), and ideal for a meal between gallery stops, take a seat at this hole-in-the-wall Osteria just off Piazza della Signoria and choose from a list of traditional Tuscan dishes neatly handwritten on a paper menu. Fresh pastas lead; try the pappardelle al cinghiale (wild boar ragu), for a truly Tuscan taste. With just a handful of tables, arrive before it fills with a hungry lunchtime crowd.

Via dei Magazzini 3r

Alla Vecchia Bettola

This corner trattoria by Piazza Tasso has an old-school trattoria feel and bustles with locals. The menu changes daily as it's incredibly seasonal with classic pastas and meats reigning; if you are chasing a bistecca, try it here. More restaurant than trattoria in price, the quality outweighs the cost and if you are seeking an authentic Tuscan dining experience, this is for you.

Vaile Vasco Pratolini 3-7

Trattoria Sostanza

Trattoria Sostanza

A hand-written menu, a limited number of seats and regular clientele offer a glimpse into Sostanza's charm, a cosy trattoria near Santa Maria Novella. Typically Tuscan in the truest sense with pastas, antipasti and mains changing daily, while its famed sizzling butter chicken is available all year round. When in season try the fluffy egg omelette with artichokes.

Via del Porcellana 25r

La Casalinga

Casalinga's name translates to 'housewife', a nod towards the quality, traditional menu. Just a skip from Piazza Santo Spirito, expect pasta hand-rolled in-house that morning tossed in a juicy ragu of rabbit or dive into a secondo dish of sliced grilled beef. Bustling all day, it's a good lunch spot in-between visits to the southern city attractions of Palazzo Pitti (see p.163) or Galleria Romanelli (see p.166).

Via dei Michelozzi 9r
www.trattorialacasalinga.it

L'Brindellone

A family-run trattoria in San Frediano, the simplicity of the dining room and classic Tuscan dishes is what makes L'Brindellone so popular with locals. It offers a weekday €10 lunch menu that includes a primo (pasta), secondo (meat dish), coffee and water, with wine from only €2 a glass. Lunch is indeed, served!

Piazza Piattellina 10–11r

NIGHTLIFE

With open-mic nights, live music, poetry and wine events, nighttime Florence is ripe for the curious and creative traveller.

Open mic at Tasso

What began as a collective of creative pals sharing their original material has grown into a popular monthly night (first Wednesday of every month) for lovers of words. Originally conceived by actress and writer, Marissa Greffy and fellow writer Lee Foust, these nights are now guest-hosted, often with a theme like 'Independence' on 4 July, so expect the creatively unexpected. Tasso also hosts regular music nights, from swing bands to body percussion acts, the line-up is eclectic and always surprising. Also see p.55.
Via Villani 15
www.tassohostelflorence.com

Le Murate

A former prison in Sant'Ambrogio, the 15th-century Le Murate was originally a convent for Benedictine nuns. Now tastefully restored into multiple cultural spaces, it features an art bar and music venue where rock bands and electro DJs perform from 9.30pm most nights (sometimes there are films or workshops instead). Be sure to check out the bathrooms in the converted jail cells. Also see p.38.
Piazza delle Murate
www.lemurate.it

L'Appartamento

Located on the first floor of a Renaissance townhouse, this literal apartment is divided into five rooms and a terrace hosting almost daily events from photography to design, artist residencies or jazz music, within its 200 square metre space. Visit Stamperia Minima, a working studio dedicated to graphic arts with engraving, woodcut and typography courses available.
Via Giraldi 11
www.appartamentofirenze.org

Open mic at Tasso

The Florentine Wine Club

The Florentine Wine Club

Run by the team behind English newspaper, *The Florentine*, their monthly
wine club is hosted by wine enthusiast and Editor-in-Chief Helen Farrell with
events at rotating wine bars across Florence. The venues present local Tuscan
wine and food producers and the Club recently branched out into showcasing
Italian craft beers. Check their website for venues each month.
www.theflorentine.net

NOF

In the heart of San Frediano, a non-descript side door leads you to this music
room where bands perform from an AstroTurf stage in the shop-front window.
The live music is free, and is on six nights a week starting from 10pm, while
beer and mixed drinks are served in its bar beneath wrought-iron fixtures and
leafy plant life.
Borgo San Frediano 17r
www.nofclub.it

Storytellers Florence

From Rome with Love: when hotel owners Linda Martinez and Steve Brenner
started Storytellers in Rome it was a lively way to gather friends, many
journalists and writers, who would share stories in their hotel garden. Its
popularity has grown such that the duo were encouraged by their Florence
followers to start a monthly night at Todo Modo (see p.35). Entry is free; sign
up to take part via their Facebook page.
Via dei Fossi 15r
www.todomodo.org

La Ménagère

Jazz at La Ménagère

Weekends have never been so hip – dive into the basement of concept store La Ménagère (see p.37) for free music nightly from Thursday to Sunday. Descend the stairs to enter a vintage club feel of the past with '50s style furniture, a small stage and candlelit tables adding a romantic touch. Under the arches is a bar serving craft cocktails to make the music, from bebop to Bossa nova, sound even sweeter.

Via de' Ginori 8r
www.lamenagere.it

La Cité

By day it is a French-inspired library-cafe popular with students. At night, La Cité turns into a hip bar serving affordable wine with live music on the ground floor. Watch folk-inspired quintets while sipping a cocktail (or hot tea), then settle into a cosy vintage seat for a late-night book reading of your choice. Not sure whether to study or go out? At La Cité you can do both.

Borgo San Frediano 20r

Circolo Aurora

Hidden in medieval Camaldoli gate, once part of the old city walls, Aurora was founded in 1946 as a social club for locals. Today it's a cocktail bar and meeting spot over two floors hosting live music, exhibitions and book readings every weekend. In the summer, its pop-up kiosk-bar's coloured tables and chairs spill into the piazza, it's popular with locals from sunset until late. Expect acoustic concerts, and DJ sets from three-piece folk outfits to double bass rhythm jazz.

Viale Vasco Pratolini 2
www.circoloaurorafirenze.it

SLEEP

From beds in a converted convent to a boudoir in a former palace, a room in a modern gallery to sleeping 'under the stars' in the largest private garden in Europe, bedtime in Florence is certainly never dull.

AdAstra

The first floor of this 15th-century palazzo has been creatively converted into 14 bedrooms by Betty Soldi and Matteo Perduca, the interiors team behind SoprArno Suites (see p.207). AdAstra has a selection of characterful rooms decorated with vintage Italian furnishings from the '50s, '60s and '70s, a mix of up-cycled furniture finished with high-end fittings – from double showers to dreamy beds, in-room bathtubs to linen so crisp you may not make it out of bed in time for breakfast.

Via del Campuccio 53
www.adastraflorence.com

Casa Howard

Having stayed at Casa Howard in Rome in the noughties, I was naturally drawn to its sister stay here in Florence. A skip from Piazza Santa Maria Novella, this boutique B&B is set within a quiet palazzo and furnished in impeccable style – modern, clean lines set against rich textiles and old-world paintings. Luxurious and utterly romantic, it's an ideal location for an overnight tête-à-tête.

Via della Scala 18
www.casahoward.com

Palazzo San Niccolò

Behind an innocuous door on a quiet backstreet of charming San Niccolò are 22 modern yet luxurious rooms within this elegant 16th-century palace. Beds are dressed with blood-red velvet headboards and throws, while the ground floor bar and lounge is chic '50s styling. The pièce de résistance is a private garden hugged by the city's medieval walls.

Via di San Niccolò 79
www.palazzosanniccolo.it

AdAstra

Milu

Milu

Milu is a boutique hotel and gallery with 22 rooms decorated in '50s retro flair yet also contemporary. Original artwork lines the walls along a grand central staircase, and also hangs in rooms – many works are for sale – while bathrooms feature a distinct pop of colour with neon perspex shower walls. Upstairs, the library shelves are lined with books dedicated to photography and the arts. The cosy terrace offers rooftop views over Florence's most fashionable street.

Via Tornabouni 8
www.hotelmilu.com

Tasso Hostel

Within a converted former school are 13 simple yet stylish rooms that make up this chic hostel. There are private double rooms with ensuite and shared dorm rooms, all tastefully decorated offering good value accommodation in the central San Frediano neighbourhood. Its tranquil courtyard is ideal on balmy nights to escape the summer city crowds. Also see p.55 and p.200.

Via Villani 15
www.tassohostelflorence.com

Gallery Hotel Art

Gallery Hotel Art prides itself on being Italy's first 'design' hotel, created by renowned Florentine architect, Michele Bönan, and owned by the famed fashion family, Ferragamo. Whitewashed walls and neutral fabrics create a serene bedroom escape by the bustle of Ponte Vecchio. It boasts a collection of art and photography and sees itself as an art gallery that accommodates cultured travellers.

Vicolo dell'Oro 5
www.lungarnocollection.com

SoprArno Suites ⬩ *Canto degli Scali*

SoprArno Suites

The former offices of *La Repubblica* newspaper were transformed into 13 themed suites in 2014 by creative couple Betty Soldi and Matteo Perduca, also of AdAstra (see p.204). Most feature in-room bathtubs plus a separate modern shower, some large enough for two. Positioned in the heart of Santo Spirito on a street lined with antique stores, their downstairs cafe SottArno (see p.83) serves as private breakfast room to hotel guests before opening to the general masses.

Via Maggio 35
www.soprarnosuites.com

Canto degli Scali

With just seven suites in a 14th-century palazzo (four apartments, three B&B), brothers Marco and Alessio Ducceschi have retained the charm of a home-away-from-home. Rooms feature wooden beams, high ceilings and terracotta floors refurbished to 21st-century luxury standards with modern kitchens and crisp linens on beds. Find it on a quiet cobbled street just minutes from Piazza della Signoria.

Via delle Terme 6
www.cantodegliscali.com

Palazzo Belfiore

When former accountant, Federico Bonechi, teamed up with sister Francesca to open seven suite Palazzo Belfiore, it was a career-change dream come true. Federico has created the ideal local stay-over, and goes further, by inviting guests, literally, into local artisan stores to meet their new neighbours. All suites have a kitchen and living space, however, as you are in hip and always happening Santo Spirito, there is a restaurant, bar or gelateria at every turn.

Via dei Velluti 8
www.palazzobelfiore.it

DAYTRIP – SIENA

A medieval city and rival to Florence for centuries, Siena is famed for its burnt-red brickwork which gives the city its warm hue. Its medieval architecture is a fascinating contrast to Florence's Renaissance buildings.

Start your day in **Piazza del Campo**, the heart of the city. Its undulating shell-like shape hosts the annual Il Palio horserace (2 July and 16 August) when the city's 17 contrade (neighbourhoods) battle it out for the prized title and a silk banner bearing the Virgin Mary. At the piazza's core is spectacular **Palazzo Pubblico** home to the commune completed in 1310 and its elegant tower, **Torre del Mangia** (Eaters Tower). Legend has it the tower was named after its first bell ringer who loved the local cuisine. Climb its 400 steps for stunning views over Siena's sweeping streets. It costs €10 (find the ticket office within the palace courtyard).

Next, get lost in the laneways heading towards Siena's **Duomo**. Wander up Via di Città which is lined with leather stores ripe with souvenirs. Stop at **Palazzo Chigi-Saracini** (no. 89), a wonderful example of Gothic architecture and peek into its ornate courtyard, now part of a music academy. Arriving at the Duomo from Via del Capitano is dazzling. Open from 10.30am the church's interior is as ornate as its facade with every inch of its walls, floor and ceiling decorated with marble and frescoes. Seek out **Piccolomini Library** with its frescoes by Pinturicchio, dedicated to Pope Pius II.

Head to Via Franciosa and lunch within the ancient caves of **Antica Osteria Da Divo** (no. 25), its dining room dating back to Etruscan times. Try the parmesan risotto, which is finished at your table, the waiter stirring your hot rice in a round of cheese to perfection.

Post-lunch, seek out Saint Catherine, the city's patron saint, who can be found, in part, within **Basilica of San Domenico**. Take a stroll around the **Fortezza** (Wednesday is market day) before an afternoon coffee stop at **Nannini** (Via Banchi di Sopra 24) to sample the classic Sienese panforte, a hard fruit and nut concoction accompanied by a stiff espresso.

GETTING THERE

Trains run every hour from Florence's main station Santa Maria Novella, taking one hour and 30 minutes. Tickets €9,30 (www.trenitalia.com). Buses depart Florence bus terminal at Santa Maria Novella every half hour, taking one hour and 15 minutes. Tickets €8,40 (www.tiemmespa.it).

Cruise the countryside in classic style. Spend a day meandering from Florence through the celebrated vineyards and idyllic Tuscan countryside of villas, cypresses and jaw-dropping vistas.

Start your day with a visit to a Medici villa. A former hunting lodge, **Villa Medicea di Lilliano** (Via Lilliano e Meoli, Grassina) is the private estate of the Malenchini family who offer wine tastings and cooking classes in their 15th-century kitchen.

Next, head further south to Radda in search of the perfect sweater at **Chianti Cashmere** (Localita' La Penisola 18) where Nora Kravis runs this tranquil goat farm creating yarn for handwoven scarves, shawls, throws and clothing.

Continue to Volpaia for lunch at **La Bottega** (Piazza Della Torre 1), run by the Barucci family who whip up quintessential Tuscan plates, some recipes are 300 years old. Sample handmade potato ravioli layered with meaty ragu or truffle tossed in tagliatelle. Much of the produce is grown in their adjoining orto (vegetable garden) with the best tables on the terrace having views towards the medieval village.

After lunch, head via **Panzano** to the ancient abbey of **Badia a Passignato**, over a thousand years old and still inhabited by monks of the Vallombrosian Order. Known for their classical and musical texts and for promoting scientific research, it's said Galileo Galilei taught here in 1587.

Heading back towards Florence, admire the architecture at **Antinori nel Chianti Classico** (Via Cassia per Siena, 133), the latest addition from the oldest wine merchants in Tuscany. Within a 1960s futuristic wood-panelled cellar, discover their history spanning 26 generations and over 600 years. In the summer, music events are held overlooking the vines. The sweeping circular staircase leads to an upper terrace for classic Chianti views.

GETTING AROUND
A Vespa is the classic way to truly explore Chianti. Hire one from €40 a day at **Florence Scooter Rental** (www.florencescooterrental.com). **Tuscany Scooter Rentals** (www.tuscanyscooterrental.com) also offer guided Vespa tours. Be sure to check your travel insurance policy for cover.

Discover the famous Five. These quaint villages are famed for bright buildings, vertiginous views and secluded swimming spots. It's a big day trip from Florence, so choose two or three villages to explore well. Here are my suggestions for what to see, do and where to eat in each village.

Start in **Riomaggiore**, the smallest village. Take the lanes up to the 13th-century fortress for spectacular views over the sea and watch the local battelli (boats) dock. **Food stops**, both on via San Giacomo: Bar Conchiglia (no. 149), Dau Cila (no. 65).

Take a boat to **Manarola** to hike its **Birolli Pass**, along the cliff and up to the cemetery on Via dei Giovani then along a small path left on Via do Corniglia into the leafy terraces with vineyards and citrus trees, finishing by San Lorenzo church. **Food stops:** Nessun Dorma (Localita Punta Bonfiglio), 5 Terre Gelateria (Via Discovolo 229).

Corniglia is the quietest village, the only one not at water level, and considered the most charming. To reach it you must take the train then climb 400 steps, with the main attractions on Via Fieschi, and **Santa Maria Belvedere** offering panoramic sea views. For the avid hiker, the path to Vernazza offers challenging terrain with spectacular views taking two hours to walk. **Food stops,** both on Via Fieschi: A Cantina da Mananan (no 117), Enoteca Il Pirun (no 115).

In **Vernazza**, take a walk to the **Doria Castle**, a 15th-century lookout (tickets €1,50) or lunch in the piazza under the colourful umbrellas facing the sea. **Food stops:** Taverna del Capitano and Gambero Rosso – both on Piazza Marconi, Belforte (Via G. Guidoni), Gelateria Amore Mio (Via Visconti, 24).

Shop in the largest village, **Monterosso** for ceramics, jewellery, clothing and food stores. Take the stairs up to the **Capuchins' monastery** and the **Church of St Francesco** to find the *Crucifixion* by Van Dyck, or swim at Fegina beach. **Food stops:** Wonderland Bakery (Via San Pietro 8), Il Golosone Gelato (Via Roma 17).

GETTING THERE

Fast trains to La Spezia Centrale from Florence's Santa Maria Novella station take two hours, 15 minutes (Tickets from €14,90). A regional service runs between villages. Research trains online at www.trenitalia.com or at the ticket office in La Spezia station. During summer, cruise ships dock in La Spezia and daytrippers descend, so if you can, visit in early spring or during autumn.

Daytrip

Known for its hilltop, stone towers, San Gimignano is an iconic sight in Tuscany. In the 14th century 72 torre (towers) filled the sky, their height was a symbol of wealth, power and prestige. Today only 13 torre remain.

Start at the gate of **San Giovanni** that dates to 1262. Wander charming **Via San Giovanni** lined with leather, linen and food stores selling spices like locally grown saffron. Once you reach **Piazza della Cisterna** you'll begin to see the famous towers.

Enter **Piazza del Duomo** and discover the magnificent **Palazzo Comunale** (Town Hall), and its facade of stone crests of past notable families. Inside, is a museum detailing San Gimignano's history and colourful 14th-century frescoes depicting town life, attributed to Memmo di Filippuccio. You can climb the tallest tower, **Torre Grossa**, at 54-metres, with the combined museum ticket. It's worth the 218 steps to see a bird's eye view of the town below. Post climb, pop into the **Duomo**, with its radiant frescoes by Bartolo do Fredi and Benozzo Gozzoli.

For lunch, grab an outside table at **Enoteca Di Vinorum** (Piazza della Cisterna 30), with stunning valley views towards Colle di Val d'Elsa. Tuck into local pecorino cheese and fennel-laced finocchiona salami washed down with a glass of Vernaccia – a white wine native to this part of Italy.

For a little shopping, visit **Matteo Macallè** (Via San Matteo 7 and 20) for handmade jewellery and **Franco Balducci** for pottery (Piazza delle Erbe 5). Then, stroll to **Rocca di Montestaffoli**, a garrison built by the Florentines in 1353. Find the remaining turret on the old walls for an alterative (free) tower climb with 360-degree views towards the Apennine Mountains. Don't miss award-winning gelato at **Dondoli**. Try Crema di Santa Fina (saffron infused with pine nuts) or zesty Champelo (grapefruit with sparkling Vernaccia wine).

Finish your visit at the **Museum of Santa Chiara**, housed in a former conservatory with an archaeological museum, herbarium and a fine contemporary art gallery, the largest in town.

GETTING THERE
Buses depart Florence bus terminal at Santa Maria Novella every hour taking one hour and 40 minutes. Tickets €6,80 (www.tiemmespa.it).

SAN GIMIGNANO PASS
A combined ticket for all civic museums including Palazzo Comunale, Torre Grossa, and Archaeological Museum. Tickets €9 (www.sangimignanomusei.it).

THE ESSENTIALS

Whether you're visiting Florence for the first time or you've discovered some of its secrets before, these tips will help you travel like a local.

GETTING TO/FROM FLORENCE

Plane

Florence has its own piccolo (little) airport, Aeroporto di Firenze-Peretola, which only a small number of airlines fly into from other European destinations. From Peretola, it's an easy taxi ride into the historic centre for a set price of €22 (plus luggage supplement) one-way.

The international airport of Tuscany is in Pisa, Galileo Galilei Airport, an hour from Florence by train. Trenitalia (www.trenitalia.com) has regular connections that will get you to Florence fast.

Train

FRECCE trains (the fast trains versus the frequent stopping regional option) are efficient and clean. Only one hour and 30 minutes to Rome from Florence, two hours to Venice or one hour and 40 minutes to Milan makes them the best way to travel between major towns and cities. Trenitalia (www.trenitalia.com) and Italo (www.italotreno.it)

offer services throughout Italy with tickets easy to purchase online. You can pre-book your seat and for FRECCE trains tickets don't need to be stamped to be validated. The conductor will ask, however, to see a copy of your booking by text, email or a paper copy.

GETTING AROUND FLORENCE

On foot

Florence is a fantastic walking city. It is small and most sites are within the old city wall circumference, and a short walk either side of the river Arno. With many streets pedestrianised, it is the easiest, fastest and most fun way to explore the city and the best way to discover little backstreets, stores and nooks you'd never otherwise find. A little tip: pack flat shoes for all those cobblestones.

Bike

Mobike (www.mobike.com), the bike sharing service, was recently introduced to Florence and with a quick sign-up via their app you can

The Essentials

hire a bike by the minute. Helmets are not required so it's an easy way to see the city should you wish to travel on two wheels. Find the nearest bike, scan its code then you're on your way.

Car

Driving in the historic centre of Florence is not advisable as it is governed by a paying system called the ZTL (zona a traffico limitato). Unless your vehicle is registered, you'll be slapped with a hefty fine if crossing into this area. Also, as streets are narrow and parking limited, it's best to avoid driving in the city centre. If you really must drive, find an official car-parking garage (normally €25 a day) that can compensate the ZTL fee for you.

If you are driving around Tuscany, remember that Italians drive on the right, and are fast drivers, especially on autostrada (tolled highways) between cities. Most of the hire car companies are based on Borgo Ognissanti in Florence and require an international driver's licence.

Bus

Buses cover the whole city from a central bus depot in Santa Maria Novella and at Piazza San Marco. Tickets (biglietti) are often purchased beforehand at a Tabbachi (newsagents) or newsstands, then stamped once you hop on board. Tickets are valid for 90 minutes.

Do remember to stamp your ticket or you could be slapped with a fine. If you have an Italian SIM card, you can text 'ATAF' to 4880105 for an electronic ticket for €1,50 versus the usual €2 price.

Taxi

Florence's taxis are white and you'll see them scooting around the central streets where they can be picked up from various official taxi ranks. Note, you are not able to flag taxis for a pick-up (you must be at a rank or pre-book one) so don't be surprised if a driver ignores your hand gesturing. Pre-booking can be done via text (+39 334 662 2550). Simply text your location then your destination and they'll send you a confirmation text with taxi name (for example ROMA 12) and the number of minutes until its arrival. Uber is banned in Florence.

LIVE LIKE A LOCAL

What to wear

Florence is an incredibly well turned-out city with people, of all ages, looking perfectly put together even to pop to the bank or a cafe. There is a sense of care and pride with quality versus quantity reigning – an Italian is more likely to buy one great cashmere sweater than ten items of fast fashion. As the seasons change you see the city's residents' uniform change too. In summer, lighter fabrics like linen are popular; come winter, coats and scarves come out in force. Ultimately the look is always polished yet comfortable. As the city is made for walking, flat shoes are recommended. For men, a smart/casual philosophy is key to fitting in with the locals with jeans, collared shirt and leather shoes a good go-to for men's style. Italians opt for a more tailored look anytime of the day.

Speak the lingua

As a tourist city, many Florentines speak English however it is best to learn a few greetings. A bright 'buongiorno' (good morning) and 'grazie' (thank you) will be appreciated. Warm and friendly, most locals will happily help you with the language barrier and you can always ask, 'parla inglese?' (Do you speak English?) or say 'non parlo Italiano' (I don't speak Italian). If in doubt, hand gestures can always help to express what you need in true Italian style.

Late nights

Florentines like to enjoy festivities into the night and in the warm summer months the city is buzzing with free outdoor concerts. My tip is to take a post-dinner night stroll to see the city's true charms. With the main streets and squares lit, come dusk it makes for a magical tour. While galleries like Palazzo Strozzi

(see p.155) offer late night Thursday open hours until 11pm each week, in summer late night gallery openings include the Uffizi Gallery (see p.147) and Palazzo Vecchio (see p.143).

Street numbers

Black versus red, residential versus business, it's easy to become confused with the street numbers in Florence. All residential buildings are numbered in black, while businesses are numbered in red and addresses finish with an 'r' (i.e. Via San Miniato 2r) for rosso (red). Street names have changed often over the centuries so don't be surprised to see two name plaques on one street corner. Using landmarks is the easiest way to navigate the city centre and when in doubt, ask a local for directions by asking where is . . . ('dov'e . . . ').

MUSEUMS

Florence has a huge number of museums and galleries, some famous, others less well known. It pays to plan visits and be in the know about passes, discounts and how to avoid the queues – especially in summertime. There used to be free entry on the first Sunday of each month to State and most civic museum however this was changed in 2018.

THE ESSENTIALS

Firenzecard

The museum pass Firenzecard (www.firenzecard.it) offers a 72-hour pass to many of the city's main attractions for €85. This allows priority access (avoid the queues!) and is also ideal for families with free admission for under 18s travelling with a Firenzecard holder. Download the app via www.firenzecard.it for the swiftest way to sign up.

Discount tickets

Some of the major museums offer discounted tickets:

Uffizi Gallery (see p.147): European Union citizens aged 18–26 are offered 50% but must show passport or ID. In winter, tickets are cheaper from November to February. Uffizi tickets also grant access to the Archaeological Museum in Piazza della Santissima Annunziata.

Palazzo Pitti (see p.163): offers a 50% discount early in the morning for tickets bought before 8.59am, and as long as you enter before 9.25am. Perfect for the Museum of Costume and Fashion (see p.165).

Duomo (see p.145): For one ticket price (€18) visit the Cathedral of Santa Maria del Fiore, Brunelleschi's Dome, Giotto's Bell Tower, the Baptistery of San Giovanni, the Crypt of Santa Reparata and the Museo dell'Opera del Duomo.

DINING IN FLORENCE

Coffee culture

In cafe bars (coffee shops are referred to as bars in Italy) there's a standing versus seating option. For on-the-go Florentines, the standing bar, overlooking the counter watching baristas whipping up their morning cappuccino, is the place to stop, drink, and then be on their way. You'll see locals eating breakfast standing with a brioche in one hand and espresso in the other. If you prefer more time off your piedi (feet), tables are available at most bars and you will be served at a table – for a price. Coffees cost around three times to sit versus stand, as you are paying for the waiting staff's charms. Note that at many cafe/bars you must first pay at the cashier then show your receipt to the counter staff in exchange for your beverage.

Time for wine

Wine is as necessary as water and a birthright for most Italians, so you will often see a couple in a piazza enjoying a glass of Prosecco at 11am or quaffing a glass of red with lunch. So join in! Wine is to be enjoyed with food and never for intoxication.

Aperitivo

Sometimes called apericena, aperitivo is essentially cocktail hour when many bars offer a selection of meats, cheeses, and hot food gratis

THE ESSENTIALS

(free) as part of your drink price. Some venues offer better quality and a more substantial selection than others and aperitivo can often become the perfect light dinner instead of a three-course meal. Come summer try a roof terrace for 'apero' with a view.

Dinner times

Italians, like many Mediterranean cultures, like to dine after sunset and in summer it's rather late for some. It's not unusual to meet for a 9pm dinner date. That's not to say you can't eat earlier – most restaurants open at 7.30pm. Dinners can be drawn out and are to be enjoyed, not rushed, so expect service to be slower than you may expect in other countries and savior the dining experience. Note that many eateries also close at 3pm between lunch and dinner service.

Florentine food

Florence's food is traditionally meat heavy because of the city's vicinity to the countryside and lack of coast, so you'll find an array of salamis and cheeses on menus. Bistecca alla Fiorentina is a famed T-bone beef steak, on average 1kg, and a dish best shared. Lightly seared on both sides then rested on the bone, it only comes one way, bloody! Yet it's not all meat on menus, with many vegetarian options popping up in recent years. Three-course feasts on menus are to be enjoyed however

are not essential – it is perfectly acceptable to simply order a primi (pasta) or secondo (meat) dish and not both.

Tipping

Although not expected tipping is always appreciated by staff so rounding up your bill a few euros if the service has been bene (good) is advisable. Some venues will add coperto (cover charge per person) and some also include a service charge, so check your bill before deciding what type of tip to leave.

SEASONS AND DATES

Florence is an exciting city all year round with street parades, contemporary art shows and fashion events to satisfy all tastes. Like all of Italy, Florence celebrates Catholic festivities, as well as historical ones. The city has become a destination for travellers all year round, the days of a quieter season a thing of the past. That said, coming in the early spring or late autumn is ideal both for the blooms, or harvest for foodies, and cooler temperatures.

January 6 – Epiphany

With a parade performed in Florence since 1417, 'Cavalcade of the Three Kings' commemorates the arrival of the three kings in Bethlehem, beginning at Palazzo Pitti and winding its way through the city

The Essentials

THE ESSENTIALS

streets with a colourful procession in Renaissance costumes. It's a public holiday, so expect many shops and offices to be closed.

Pitti Immagine

This bi-annual fashion spectacle in June and January (check website for dates www.pittimmagine.com), means the city is inundated with fashion industry movers and shakers from around the world keen to spy the latest menswear collections. The trade shows are ticketed however there are a huge amount of events open to the public with pop-up shops, bars and street parties taking place all week. In March, Pitti Taste, a foodie version of the festa, is hosted.

February 18 – Anna Maria Luisa de' Medici

Anna Maria Luisa de' Medici, credited with preserving Florence's art and culture, an esteemed Fiorentina, is celebrated every February with free entrance to the civic museums through the city and an opportune day to explore Palazzo Vecchio (see p.143) or Bargello.

March 25 Florentine New Year

The Renaissance capital has its own New Year celebrated nine months before Christ's birth – Feast of the Annunciation – when Angel Gabriel informed Mary she was soon to be with child. A morning parade from Piazza della Signoria to Piazza della Santissima Annunziata is a spectacle, while an outdoor food market runs in Annunziata until 5pm.

Easter Scoppio del Carro

The biggest holiday in the Christian calendar, Florence hosts an explosive spectacle in Piazza del Duomo at 11am on Easter Sunday. The city's celebrations date back 1000 years to the First Crusade. Since the 15th century, a richly decorated cart travels through the streets after mass before being lit with multi-colored fireworks exploding to symbolise the next year's harvest.

May Maggio Musicale

One of the oldest and most important music festivals in Europe was founded in Florence in 1933 and every year during May, shows are performed in theatres throughout the city including state-of-the-art opera house, Teatro dell'Opera di Firenze. Find performance and ticket details at www.maggiofiorentino.com

June 24 – Calcio Storico and St John's Day

Celebrating Florence's patron saint, San Giovanni (St John) coincides with the final of the historic soccer match, Calcio Storico. A mix of rugby, soccer and boxing, Calcio Storico is played between the four old quartiere of the city in Piazza di Santa Croce before the winning team takes to the streets in celebration of their win. Come nightfall, the city sets off a fireworks display at 10pm from Ponte Vecchio (see p.149) in honour of St John.

August holidays

Summertime sees a heatwave strike Florence and is when the locals flock to the nearest beach. During August many of the independent stores close for the whole month and you'll find the quieter backstreets void of their usual buzz. The main museums and galleries all continue to open their doors, so the city hotspots are as vibrant as ever. Expect temperatures in the high 30°C range and take advantage of a siesta to avoid the midday sun.

December 8 – Christmas lights

There is something serene and magical about the twinkle of soft white lights around Florence in December. Piazza Santa Croce hosts an annual Christmas market in traditional German style, while the annual Christmas tree in Piazza del Duomo is lit on December 8 to much city fanfare.

PRACTICALITIES

Wi-Fi

You can find Wi-Fi in most cafes and the city also offers a free service: 'Firenze WiFi' to log on to. If staying more than a few days, grabbing an Italian SIM at one of the TIM stores is an easy, and affordable, way to stay connected on your travels.

GRAZIE MILLE!

Thank you Hardie Grant for believing in Lost in Florence *from the very start: Melissa Kayser for reaching out with the idea and Megan Cuthbert and Alice Barker for their wonderful editorial insights. Thank you to Lila Theodoros for your incredible design.*

My Florence belle – Nancy Disk, Esther Millenaar, Sofie Delauw, Jen Warakomski, Camilla Jackson and Sarah Adams, Italian life wouldn't be the same without you. My Gucci girls – Alexandra Lawrence, Georgette Jupe Pradier and Lisa Condie, from the start you were a huge support. Betty Soldi for being my champion from the very beginning. Eric Veroliemeulen and Andrina Richards Lever for your endless encouragement and enthusiasm.

The countless artisans and shopkeepers, bartenders and restaurateurs, who have opened their Florentine doors and invited me into their stores. Thank you for sharing your stories with me.

The collective of incredible photographers who have contributed to these pages – grazie! This book would not be the same without your involvement and beautiful images.

PP for being by my side especially during my writing days – ti amo.

And my family who have always encouraged me to travel and follow my dreams, all the crazy ideas that involve foreign lands, exotic food and memories that will last a lifetime.

Published in 2019 by Hardie Grant Travel, a division of Hardie Grant Publishing

Hardie Grant Travel (Melbourne)
Building 1, 658 Church Street
Richmond, Victoria 3121

Hardie Grant Travel (Sydney)
Level 7, 45 Jones Street
Ultimo, NSW 2007

www.hardiegrant.com.au/travel

A catalogue record for this Book is available from the National Library of Australia

Lost in Florence
ISBN 9781741176360

10 9 8 7 6 5 4 3 2 1

Publisher
Melissa Kayser
Senior editor
Megan Cuthbert
Project editor
Alice Barker
Editorial assistance
Rosanna Dutson
Proofreader
Alison Proietto
Design
Lila Theodoros
Prepress by Megan Ellis and Splitting Image Colour Studio

Printed and bound in China by LEO Paper Group

All photos © Nardia Plumridge, except the following:
(Letters indicate where multiple images appear on a page, from top to bottom, left to right)
Front cover: Olga Makarova
Back cover: Andrea Palei (a); Sei Divino (b); Tracy Russo (c)(e)(j); Marina Denisova (g)(k); Olga Makarova (h); Anna Positano (i); Gucci (l)
Alessandro Moggi 30, 154; Alessio Dipaola 26, 58; Alina Krasieva 78; Andrea Palei 86; Anna Positano 40; Antinori 64; Beatrice Mancini 39, 50(b), 71, 84, 88, 92, 112, 120, 121, 128, 138, 162, 164, 184, 186, 194; Braciere Malatesta 70, 193; Burro e Acciughe 87; Christine Juette 33(c), 38, 43, 134, 184; Claudio Pulicati 114; David Glauso 177; Emiko Davies 214; Enrico Lanari 21, 157; Eric Veroliemeulen 102, 156; Eva Vujacic Photography 110(a)(b)(d); Fondazione Franco Zeffirelli 160; Francesca Sara Cauli 170(a), 193, 195; Gabriel Preda 44; Giovanni Rasoti 48; Giovanni Savi 97; Gucci 62, 152; Guglielmo de' Micheli 179; Ilaria Costanzo 28, 122, 170(c), 178, 184, 187, 191, 205, 207(a); John Werich 210; Lorenzo Papi 166; Lorenzo Villoresi 170(b); Marcela Schneider Ferreira 110(c); Marina Denisova 56, 82; Matteo Del Re 42; Mercato Centrale Firenze 66; Morgan O'Donovan 206; MUS.E Firenze 168; Museo Salvatore Ferragamo 150; Naomi Muirhead 104; Olga Makarova vi, 2, 5, 52, 53, 65, 80, 98, 100, 101, 124, 146, 148(a); Ostello Tasso 54, 201; Pescepane 72; Procacci 32; Raffaello Romanelli 166; Sam Andruszkiewicz 96; Samantha Stout 68; Sei Divino 33(a)(b), 186; Simone Bartoletti 177; Sofie Delauw ii-iii, 36, 46, 60, 74, 79, 103, 118, 119, 126, 130, 197, 198, 199, 203, 216(b), 224; Stewart Szervo 136; Studio Fotografico Firenze 207(b); The Finest Food In Florence 193; Todo Modo 34; Tommaso Ferri 106, 131; Tracy Russo 10, 208, 142, 144, 158, 216(a); Yuri Pozzi 129; Shutterstock 213

Florence map and illustrations © Shutterstock 2019